Landscapes of
BRITTANY
a countryside guide

Rodney Ansell

SUNFLOWER
BOOKS

Dedicated to Yvette, who was one of the gang

First published 1993 by
Sunflower Books
12 Kendrick Mews
London SW7 3HG, UK

ISBN 1-85691-025-3

Important note to the reader ___

I have tried to ensure that the descriptions and maps in this book are error-free at press date. The book will be updated, where necessary, whenever future printings permit. It will be very helpful for me to receive your comments (sent in care of the publishers, please) for the updating of future printings. I also rely on those who use this book — especially walkers — to take along a good supply of common sense when they explore. Conditions can change fairly rapidly, and **storm damage or bulldozing may make a route unsafe at any time.** If the route is not as outlined here, and your way ahead is not secure, return to the point of departure. **Never attempt to complete a tour or walk under hazardous conditions!** Please read carefully the notes on pages 10, 46, and 47, as well as the introductory comments at the beginning of each tour and walk (regarding road conditions, equipment, grade, distances and time, etc). Explore **safely**, while at the same time respecting the beauty of the countryside.

Cover photograph: Château de Trédion
Title page: La Roche aux Fées
Above: 'Gargantua's Finger', with Forte La Latte in the background

Photographs by the author
Touring map by John Theasby and Pat Underwood
Walking maps adapted from IGN Série Bleue 1:25,000 maps of Brittany, with permission of the Institut Géographique Nationale
Drawings by John Theasby
Printed and bound in the UK by Brightsea Press, Exeter

Contents

Preface	4
Grande Randonnée; Acknowledgements; Useful books; Maps	
Introduction	6
How to get there; Getting about; Weather; Where to stay; Breton customs and culture	
A country code for walkers and motorists	10
Picnicking and picnic suggestions	11
Touring	16
1 Léon	17
2 Armorican Natural Park	23
3 Cornouaille	27
4 Western Morbihan	31
5 Eastern Morbihan	35
6 Côtes-d'Armor	39
7 The Chateaubriand road	42
Walking	46
WALKS IN FINISTERE	
... in Léon	
1 Parish closes of St-Thégonnec and Guimiliau	48
... in the Armorican Natural Park	
2 Pointe de Pen-Hir	52
3 Morgat — pearl of the Crozon	57
4 Forest of Huelgoat	61
5 Ménez-Hom	65
6 In the Arrée Hills	70
7 Ménez-Mikel	72
8 Through the valley of the Elorn	75
... in Cornouaille	
9 The Grande Troménie	78
10 Penmarc'h	83
11 Pointe du Raz	86
12 In Gauguin's footsteps	90
WALKS IN MORBIHAN	
13 The menhirs of Carnac	93
14 Josselin Castle and the Sedon Valley	97
15 The chapels of Le Faouët	101
16 Beside the river Blavet	106
WALKS IN ILLE-ET-VILAINE	
17 Le Val sans Retour	110
18 Forest of Paimpont	113
WALKS IN COTES-D'ARMOR	
19 Dinan	116
20 Bon-Repos Abbey and Quénécan Forest	122
21 The Pink Granite Coast	127
Bus and train timetables	133
Index	135
Touring map	between pages 16 and 17

Preface

The great glory of Brittany is its coastline. Other parts of France may have high mountains and wide moors, but nowhere can match Brittany for its shores. Deeply indented, they twist and wind for more than 1000 kilometres (700 miles), constantly varied and continually breathtaking — from the sun-warmed beaches of La Baule, via the mysterious, almost enclosed sea of Morbihan and the (sometimes) storm-battered and totally untouched shores of Finistère, to the dramatically beautiful Pink Granite Coast with its myriad off-shore islets.

The interior is no less beautiful, filled with interest for the visitor: the Arrée Hills and Black Mountains of Finistère, the ancient forests of Huelgoat and Paimpont, the great canal that Napoleon dug from Brest to Nantes to avoid the British Royal Navy, and a host of picturesque villages and historic towns. All of the tours and walks in this book help you enjoy Brittany to the full.

A word about the spelling of place names. I have generally used the spellings shown on the IGN maps (see next page) but, in the text, I have mentioned some of the many signposts that bear spellings quite different from

---

Grande Randonnée

One of the great joys of walking in France is the existence of the footpaths of the Grande Randonnée. The Grande Randonnée comprises a series of long distance footpaths which traverse the country's most scenic regions. Brittany has hundreds of miles of them. The route is exhaustively waymarked with white and red markers at frequent intervals. There are advance warnings given of a change of direction, arrows showing that you must now turn to the right or the left, and crosses to show that you have failed to notice a change of direction and are going the wrong way. Brittany has many local walks (Petites Randonnées) as well. Good as it may be, their waymarking serves only to show the superlative nature of that of the Grande Randonnée.

Carefully chosen, the GR routes meander across the countryside to visit every point of interest in the neighbourhood, seeking out farm tracks and paths to get you away from the tarmac road, and constantly deviating to bring you the best viewpoints. The care and thought that has gone into the planning of these routes is extraordinary and, wherever possible, the walks in this book follow them.

I guarantee that, when you have walked a few sections of the Grande Randonnée, you will fall in love with it … and that, as you drive across France, whenever through the car window you see the familiar white and red blaze, you will feel a barely-resistible urge to stop the car, get out and follow wherever it may lead.

those shown on the maps. These variations can be quite confusing, so be aware of them when comparing maps with signposts.

Acknowledgements

I must record my gratitude to all who have helped with the preparation of this book:

my wife, Helen, for her willingness to put up with my long absences and readiness to act as guinea-pig and photographer's assistant;

Yvette, who devoted her holiday to trying out the walks, and whose dedication went far beyond the call of duty; Gareth, who saw me through the pitfalls of word processing (and who lent me my own car for six weeks!), and Martin, for much helpful advice gleaned from countless Boy Scout and Duke of Edinburgh's Award hikes;

Brittany Ferries and their staff, especially Toby Oliver, Sarah Bensted-Smith and Sasha Hancock;

McCarta Ltd, and Mike Chapman in particular;

the staff of countless tourist information offices across Brittany, and Fabienne Le Goff of the C.R.T.B. Rennes;

the many hoteliers who not only provided excellent hospitality and cuisine, but went out of their way to help with such mundane matters as drying my laundry, and who imparted much useful information about the locality, of whom my special thanks go to Serge Quillec and his mother of the Hôtel de la Gare, Pleyber-Christ, and Françoise Jèzèquel of La Chaumière Hotel in Gourin.

Useful books
Available in England
The Rough Guide to Brittany & Normandy, Greg Ward (Rough Guides). Useful for choosing your resort and greral information.

Tourist Guide — Brittany (Michelin). Invaluable; if it's worth knowing, it's included.

Available in France
A useful, extensive series of mini-guides published by Ouest-France is available to French readers in all bookshops in Brittany, covering every aspect of the province. The following titles are also available in English/German:

The Alignments of Carnac, P.-R. Giot; *Roman Art in Brittany*, M. Renouard; *Brittany*, M. Renouard; *Carnac*, C. Le Quintrec; *The Castle of Josselin*, A. de Rohan; *Locronan*, M. Dilasser; *Saint-Malo*, H. Queffélec; *Tréguier*, M. Devillers; *Guimiliau*, E. Royer (only in German); *Pleyben*, A. Legrand (only in German); *Saint-Thégonnec*, P. Derrien (only in German).

Maps
For motoring
1:250 000 IGN Red Series number 105

1:100 000 IGN Green Series numbers 13, 14, 15, 16

1:200 000 Michelin Yellow Maps numbers 58, 59, 63 or Michelin Motoring Atlas of France

For walking
The IGN Blue Series maps reproduced in this book (reduced from their original scale of 1:25 000 to 1:40 000) should be ample for a month's walking holiday. Should you wish to go further afield, see the IGN catalogue.

Introduction

Long ago Brittany comprised 'the Sea' (ar Mor) and 'the Forest' (ar Goat), and the people lived in the coastal strip of ar Mor. So when Julius Caesar conquered the land for Rome, he called it 'Gallia Armorica'. After the Romans pulled out of northern Europe in the fifth century, Armorica became home to so many British refugees that the French dubbed it 'Little Britain' (Bretagne), and the name has stuck ever since. Virtually cut off from the rest of France by wilderness, Brittany was practically an independent state until its last ruler, Duchess Anne, married the French king in 1491, and Brittany became swallowed up in France. Even so, its isolation was only ended with the coming of the railway in the nineteenth century. But there has been one lasting link between the duchy and the rest of France throughout history. Brittany has always supplied France with its sailors.

How to get there

In general the most satisfactory approach from England is by the Brittany Ferries car ferry from Plymouth to Roscoff for western Brittany, or Portsmouth to St-Malo for eastern Brittany. From Ireland there is a weekly boat from Cork to Roscoff. Shorter crossings which involve travelling across northern France may be made by various ferries and hovercraft to the other Channel ports.

It is possible to fly from London (Gatwick) to Brest, Nantes, Rennes and Quimper, and from Cork to Morlaix during the summer; also from London (Heathrow) to Nantes throughout the year. These flights are considerably more expensive than the boats. It might be cheaper to fly to Paris and go on by train.

Getting about

A good railway service circles the province and links the main towns, connecting with an excellent bus service to take you into the interior, or on to your coastal resort. Bus timetables are given at the end of this book (page 133) to enable you to reach the starting point for the walks. If possible, use the local tourist information office (nearly every town has one) to confirm that they are still up-to-date. However, do bear in mind that Brittany is a very large holiday region, and the times involved in travelling about by train and bus can be quite considerable.

Cars can be hired in the towns, and bicycles at many of the railway stations. Bicycles can also travel free as hand luggage on many of the local trains, provided there is room in the luggage van. In addition, 700km (400 miles) of navigable rivers and canals criss-cross the province, and every kind of craft can be hired from a score of firms. There are also boat excursions to the many islands, to explore the Morbihan Gulf, along the Rance from Dinard or St-Malo to Dinan, and between Quimper and Bénodet.

Weather

Brittany is mild in winter and not unpleasantly hot in summer. It is, however, the wettest region of France and, although July and August are the driest months, it is essential, even in high summer, to provide yourself with good waterproof clothing. On the whole the south coast is the driest part, and the west coast the windiest. For the walker this is not all bad news. If you are well protected, the rain scarcely detracts from a good walk, the winds can blow up very exciting seas off Finistère and, best of all, the uncertain weather has kept much of the coastline of Brittany undeveloped, so that on the many warm and calm days in early or late summer, you can have mile upon mile of some of the most gorgeous beaches and cliffs in Europe virtually to yourself.

Where to stay

Hotels of every category, campsites and *gîtes* (holiday cottages) abound, inland as well as around the coast. The two large commercial towns of Brest and Lorient are perhaps best avoided, otherwise you have a choice of every kind of centre, from the sophisticated resorts of La Baule and Dinard, through lively sea-side towns like Perros-Guirec and Bénodet, to historic ones such as Dinan and Quimper, as well as hundreds of friendly little villages.

All accommodation is at a premium during the short season of July and August. If you are holidaying in these months, you would be well advised to reserve rooms in advance at the sea-side and to arrive at campsites and inland hotels at midday, when there will almost always be vacancies created by people moving on. The necessity to provide ample accommodation for the short summer season ensures that there will always be a surfeit outside those months, when you will also often get better terms and a greater choice.

B reton customs and culture

From time immemorial the inhabitants of Brittany have been of a devoutly religious disposition. It has found its outward expression in certain customs, monuments, and buildings that have given the region a unique character.

Pardons

Brittany's version of the religious festival, the *pardon* was originally linked with penitence and forgiveness. But is by no means a gloomy affair, rather a statement of traditional values and a chance to wear the national costume — including the famous *coiffes* or head-dresses of the women. The characteristic feature of the *pardon* is a procession around the parish.

Plas ar Horn, the most sacred place of pilgrimage on the Grande Troménie. Walk 9 follows in part the route of this famous pardon.

Megalithic monuments

Long before the coming of the Gauls, a people sailed across the Bay of Biscay and settled on the southern shore of Brittany. They brought with them a highly-developed cult of the dead. Their great stone ('megalithic') monuments are found everywhere in the province, but most abundantly in the vicinity of Carnac. You will encounter several sorts of monument; their erection spans an era of many hundreds of years.

Menhir: The menhir (photograph page 20) is a single upright stone, venerated until the coming of Christianity, and occasionally 'Christianised' by the addition of a cross.

Alignment: A line of menhirs. Sometimes, as at Carnac (photograph page 96), several parallel lines are found, with hundreds of stones.

Cromlech: A circle of menhirs.

Dolmen: Two upright stones, with a third one balanced on top to make a roof (photograph page 82). Now usually exposed, it was originally covered with earth or stones, and used as a burial chamber.

Allée couverte: The 'covered alley' or gallery grave is an extended dolmen: two rows of stones supporting roofing stones. Like the dolmen, it was used as a burial chamber, but superstition saw both as the dwellings of fairies and dwarfs (see drawing of 'La Roche aux Fées' on title page).

Tumulus: A dolmen or *allée couverte* still covered with earth or stones, creating an artificial mound. When it is covered only with stones, it is sometimes called a cairn.

Wayside crosses

Nowhere in the world do so many crosses and calvaries (photograph page 71) stand beside the road (most often at junctions) as in Brittany. They seem to continue a tradition begun long ago by the builders of the menhirs. Before the days of proper roads, amongst other functions, they would act as signposts — indicating for example the route of *pardons*.

Wells

In antiquity it was not unusual for springs to be regarded with reverence, as being the homes of gods or water sprites. In Brittany this reverence has never died out. The clergy tamed it by dedicating the wells to Christian saints, often building a chapel near by. The Bretons' continuing affection for their wells can be seen in the way they are still lovingly tended, often surrounded with flowers. See photograph page 99.

Parish closes

Four features make up the 'parish close': the church, the lych-gate ('triumphal arch'), the charnel-house ('ossuary'), and the crucifix ('calvary').

Churches: For most of its history Brittany was quite extraordinarily poor. The traditional livelihood of its men was the sea and, in the 16th century, this began to pay off. Wealth spread inland from the sailors to the farmers who, having little else to spend their money on, devoted it to the elaboration of their parish churches. Most of the churches you will see date from this time (photographs pages 65, 79). They are mostly Gothic (even though elsewhere in Europe a classical revival was taking place), with the windows decorated in a peculiarly French style known as *flamboyant*, from its curiously flame-like effect. The pride of every Breton church is its belfry, and no parish wished to be outdone by its neighbour. Also on the exterior, notice the porch; this served as the village council chamber, hence the stone benches. What gives these porches their special character are the rows of apostles which frequently line the walls. The interior of many churches will be dominated by a rood-screen, often richly carved and painted. All of this was the work of Breton craftsmen, and there is to it a homely, almost naive approach that is most appealing.

Triumphal arch: The gateway to the churchyard was developed in classical style, reaching its zenith in the magnificent *arcs de triomphe* at Sizun (photograph page 24) and Pleyben.

Ossuary: Death has never been far from the Breton consciousness since the days of the megalith builders. Bones disinterred from graveyards (to make room for the newly-deceased) were stored in these charnel houses, which were also rebuilt on the grand scale (see below). Most are now used as souvenir shops, but you may occasionally come across one, as in Guéhenno (Car tour 5), that still has the chill of death upon it.

Calvary: See photograph page 60. The practice of adding the figures of St Mary and St John to the statue of the crucified Christ is not uncommon, as too is the addition of the crucified robbers. Brittany goes much, much further than this. Everybody connected with Christ's passion gets a place. At times it seems as though everybody in the New Testament is there … as well as Katel-Gollet ('Catherine the Lost'). She was a Breton serving-girl thrown into hell for stealing a consecrated host to give to her lover, alas none other than the Devil.

Ossuary at Sizun

A country code for walkers and motorists

The experienced rambler is used to following a 'country code', but the holiday-maker out for a stroll may unwittingly cause damage, harm animals, and even endanger his own life. Do heed this advice:

- **Do not light fires**. Even in Brittany things can get tinder-dry in summer. Be especially vigilant in the forests.
- **Do not frighten animals**.
- **Walk quietly** through all farms, hamlets and villages, **leaving all gates just as you found them**. They are there to keep animals (or children) in — or out of — an area. Remember, too, that a gate may be of a temporary nature (brushwood or cord across a path), but it serves the same purpose, so please replace it after passing.
- **Protect all wild and cultivated plants**. Don't try to pick wild flowers or uproot saplings. When photographing wild flowers, watch where you put your feet so that you do not destroy others in the process. Obviously fruit and crops are someone's private property and should not be touched.
- **Never walk over cultivated land**.
- **Take all your litter away with you**.
- Walkers — **do not take risks**. Review the 'Important note to the reader' on page 2 and the notes for walkers on pages 46 and 47. Do not attempt walks beyond your capacity and **never walk alone**. *Always* tell a responsible person exactly where you are going and what time you plan to return. Remember, if you become lost or injure yourself, it may be a long time before you are found. On any but a very short walk near to villages, it's a good idea to take along a torch, a whistle, a compass, extra water and warm clothing

	SENTIER GR	SENTIER GR DE PAYS	SENTIER PR
CONTINUITÉ DU SENTIER			
CHANGEMENT DE DIRECTION			
MAUVAISE DIRECTION			

GR ('Grande Randonnée) waymarks are white/red; the 'GR du Pays' (regional walk) waymarks are white/yellow; PR or 'Petite Randonnée' (local walk) waymarks are yellow. Where there are a number of local walks in the vicinity, a variety of colours will be used. Top row: 'continue this way'; middle row: 'change of direction'; bottom row 'wrong way'.

Picnicking

In so large and beautiful a region as Brittany, picnicking possibilities are virtually limitless. In addition to natural settings (the whole west coast of Finistère can be seen as one vast picnic site, as can the banks of its canalised rivers), there are many organised sites beside the roads (indicated in the touring notes and on the touring map with the symbol ⊼. Below are a few of the sites that I think you may especially enjoy visiting. All the information you need to visit them is given on the following pages, where 🚌 = how to get there by bus; 🚗 = car or taxi parking.

All of my picnic suggestions are accessible in the course of the car tours: these are highlighted on the *touring* map with the symbol ***P***. Some lie along walking routes, and their location is shown on the corresponding *walking* map by the ***P*** symbol. Although 'off the beaten track', they are quite easily accessible and offer a reasonable amount of space for you to spread out without being in the way of passers-by, a pleasant view and, where possible, something firm and dry to sit on, whether rocks or benches.

1 LE CONQUET (Car tour 1; touring map) ⊼

by bus: 20min on foot   *by car: no walking*
🚌 to Le Conquet from Brest, then walk back along the Brest road for 1.5km/1mi to this organised picnic site, on your left.
🚗 Either follow Car tour 1 as far as this picnic site outside Le Conquet, or drive along the D789 from Brest to Le Conquet, stopping just short of the village.
The site is in attractive scenery and well provided with tables. For an informal site by the sea, choose the rocky coast between Le Conquet and the Pointe de St-Mathieu, beside the D85 (adequate parking). Times would be little different from those given above for the organised site.

2 TREGLONOU (Car tour 1; touring map) ⊼

only accessible by car: no walking
🚗 Follow Car tour 1 as far as the Aber Benoît estuary. The picnic site is in the hamlet of Tréglonou. Or drive north from Brest on the D13 and turn left about 3km/2mi south of Lannilis.
A pleasantly situated site above the estuary of the Aber Benoît.

3 LOCQUENOLE (Car tour 1; touring map) ⊼

only accessible by car: no walking
🚗 Follow Car tour 1 as far as the Rade de Morlaix. The site is 3km/2mi south of the junction with the D73, just north of Locquénolé. Or drive northwards from Morlaix beside the river for 8km/5mi, firstly on D769, and then on D73, in the direction of Carantec. Park by the site.
Magnificent views over the estuary of the river Morlaix.

4 CAMARET (Car tour 2; Walk 2; map page 54) ⊼

by bus: 10min on foot   *by car: 10min on foot*

🚌 to Camaret. Walk to the end of the harbour and turn left to walk up the hill behind the beach, to a grassy picnic site.

🚐 Follow Car tour 2 to Camaret. Park in the town centre, next to the harbour, and follow the notes for bus passengers above.

After your picnic, leave the site by the top right-hand corner, for access to the beach and cliffs.

5 ANSE DE PEN-HAT (Car tour 2; Walk 2; map page 54) ⊼

by bus: 30min on foot   *by car: no walking*

🚌 to Camaret. Walk nearly to the seaward end of the harbour, then turn left, following the sign for the Pointe de Pen-Hir. Take the first road on the right, and follow it for 1.3km/0.8mi, keeping left at the junction halfway along, to where a road on the left leads to a car park. Or follow the beginning of Walk 2, for a slightly longer and more interesting stroll.

🚐 Follow Car tour 2 to Camaret. Turn left at the end of the port for the Pointe de Pen-Hir, and follow the notes for bus passengers above.

Beyond the car park there is a small picnic area (only two tables). There is no shade, but the scenery is magnificent. Or go down to the beach. There are rocks if you want somewhere firm to sit.

6 LOST MARC'H (Car tour 2; Walk 3; map page 58; photo page 57)

only accessible by car: 8min on foot

🚐 Drive to Morgat. Follow the D887 for two-thirds of the way round the bay, then turn right. Drive through the hamlet of Tréflez and follow the road westwards, until it peters out in Lost Marc'h. Park here, and follow the track ahead to the Pointe de Lost Marc'h.

The coast here offers innumerable places for an informal picnic.

7 HUELGOAT (Car tour 2; Walk 4; map page 62; photo page 60) ⊼

by bus: 15min on foot   *by car: 20min on foot*

🚌 to Huelgoat. Walk down to the lake and turn right. Follow the shore to the end, then turn left in front of the Café du Chaos. After 50m/yds take the first road on the right, signposted 'La Roche Tremblante'. Just before the top of the hill, turn right along a similarly-signposted path. Follow it to steps leading to a huge rock, beyond which there is a picnic area. Return to the town by turning right and walking beside the stream, along the Sentier des Amoureux.

🚐 Drive to Huelgoat which is just north of the D764 Carhaix to Morlaix road, and park beside the lake. On leaving the car park, with your back to the lake, turn left, then follow the notes for bus passengers above.

Huelgoat is a very pretty place, with many short forest walks along marked paths. A visit is strongly recommended.

8 MENEZ-HOM (Car tour 2; Walk 5; map pages 66-67)

by bus: at least 1h30min on foot   *by car: no walking*

🚌 to St-Nic. From the bus stop, walk into the village, pass the church on your left, and turn up the first road on the right. After 0.5km/0.3mi keep left at the fork and, 200m/yds further on, pass a road on the left. Keep ahead when the tarmac turns to gravel track. Bear left at the junction with a tarmac road, then turn right at the junction with the D887. Take the first road on the left, the D83, and continue the climb to the summit of Ménez-Hom.

🚐 Turn right off the D887 (Châteaulin to Crozon road), up the D83, and drive to the car park at the summit of Ménez-Hom.

The gently-rounded summit of one of Brittany's highest hills offers panoramic views over the countryside. Only suitable on calm days.

9 MENEZ-MIKEL (Car tour 2; Walk 7; map page 73; photo page 74)

only accessible by car: no walking

🚗 Turn off the D785 (Morlaix to Quimper road) 6.5km/4mi north of Brasparts and drive up a country lane to the car park at the summit of St Michael's Mount (Ménez-Mikel/Mont St-Michel).

On a calm day, the summit of the loftiest of the Breton hills will provide you with ample space to picnic and fine views over the Yeun Elez bog, reservoir, and nuclear power station.

10 ST-GUENOLE (Car tour 3; Walk 10; map page 84) 🎏

by bus: 15min on foot   *by car: no walking*

🚌 to St-Guénolé, near Penmarc'h. From the centre of St-Guénolé follow signs for the 'Musée', walking parallel with the coast, until you come to the Musée de Préhistoire. There is a small picnic area adjacent to the museum, or sit on the magnificent beach.

🚗 Follow Car tour 3 to St-Guénolé, or take the D785 southwest from Quimper to Penmarc'h. On the outskirts of Penmarc'h, fork right on the D53 for St-Guénolé. After about 1.7km/1mi turn right for the Musée de Préhistoire. There is parking and a picnic area next to it.

The site is at the start of one of the longest beaches in Europe, interrupted only by the Pointe de la Torche, which you see in the distance. Totally undeveloped, this beach is deserted for most of the year.

11 AUDIERNE (Car tour 3; touring map) 🎏

by bus: 30min on foot   *by car: no walking*

🚌 to Audierne. Head north from the village on the D765, in the direction of Pont-Croix, walking beside the Goyen estuary.

🚗 Follow Car tour 3 to the outskirts of Audierne, or drive along D765 from Douarnenez.

A small site with tables and benches, overlooking the Goyen estuary.

12 ST-NICOLAS-DES-EAUX (Car tour 4; touring map) 🎏

only accessible by car: no walking

🚗 Follow Car tour 4 to St-Nicolas-des-Eaux, or join the D1 to St-Nicholas by turning west off the D768 (Baud to Pontivy road) 8.5km/5.3mi north of Baud. Cross the river and turn right to the picnic area.

This interesting and beautiful spot, at the bottom of the Blavet Valley, is deservedly popular. There are exceptional views from the summit of the hill.

Mill at Hugelgoat (Car tour 2, Walk 4, Picnic 7)

13 LAKE GUERLEDAN (Car tour 4; touring map) ⌂

by bus: up to 15min on foot   *by car: no walking*

🚌 to St-Gelven from Carhaix or Loudéac. Walk back towards the lake.
🚗 Follow Car tour 4, or drive 8km/5mi west from Mur-de-Bretagne on the N164. The attractive, well-equipped site is south of the main road.
Overlooks Lake Guerlédan, with the Forest of Quénécan beyond.

14 ST-FIACRE (Car tour 4; Walk 15; map page 105) ⌂

by bus: 30min on foot   *by car: no walking*

🚌 to Le Faouët. Stand in the middle of the market square, with your back to the ancient covered market, and leave by the right-hand corner, keeping straight ahead and passing the old chapel (now the tourist information office) on your right. Follow the street due south for 1.5km/1mi, then fork left along a track and continue southwards for 450m/0.3mi. Cross a road and go down a short track opposite, to arrive at the lovely chapel of St-Fiacre with its adjoining picnic area.
🚗 Follow Car tour 4, or drive to Le Faouët. On reaching the market square, follow signs for Scaër, Quimperlé and St-Fiacre. After 3km/1.9mi bear left to the chapel of St-Fiacre.
The lovely chapel makes a splendid backdrop to this rural site.

15 BON-REPOS (Car tour 4; Walk 20; map page 123; photographs pages 24, 125) ⌂

by bus: 5min on foot   *by car: no walking*

🚌 to Bon-Repos from Carhaix or Loudéac. Walk south to the abbey.
🚗 Follow Car tour 4, or turn south off the N164 (Carhaix to Loudéac road) 5km/3mi east of Gouarec. In quiet surroundings, the picnic area lies between the river Daoulas and the ruins of the abbey of Bon-Repos.
Not only do you have the ruined abbey to explore, but you have the choice of several short strolls beside the river Blavet, in the Forest of Quénécan, or along the Gorges du Daoulas.

16 LOCMARIAQUER (Car tour 4; touring map) ⌂

only accessible by car: no walking

🚗 Follow Car tour 4 to Locmariaquer, or drive south from Auray on the D28. Once in the village, follow signs for 'Plages'. After about 1.7km/1mi you will find a shaded picnic area with tables and a splendid view over the Bay of Quiberon. Nearby is the dolmen of Pierres-Plats. Alternatively, follow signs for 'Pointe de Kerpenhir', where there is an equally delightful picnic area beneath trees, with views over the Morbihan narrows.There are no tables at Pointe de Kerpenhir, however.
Locmariaquer overlooks the Gulf of Morbihan and is the starting port for boats which visit the islands or tour the inland sea. At low tide the shores of the gulf are the feeding ground for many varieties of birds, including herons and little egrets.

17 JOSSELIN (Car tour 5; Walk 14; map page 100) ⌂

by bus: 5min on foot   *by car: 5min on foot*

🚌 to Josselin. On the opposite side of the main road from the back of the castle there is a park with a picnic area, separated from the 'Parking d'Aiguillon' by a stream.
🚗 Follow Car tour 5, or drive on the N24 to Josselin. Coming from the west, drive between the castle and the river,and carry on to the next T-junction, where a car park (the 'Parking d'Aiguillon') faces you. Coming from the east, at the bottom of the hill, as you enter the town, the 'Parking d'Aiguillon' is on your right, at the point where you first draw level with the castle wall. The picnic area is separated from the car park by a stream.

Besides picnicking in a delightful little park, you have the opportunity to explore this historic town, with its famous castle, and walk along the bank of the river Oust.

18 PAIMPONT (Car tour 5; touring map) ⊼

only accessible by car: no walking

🚗 Drive to Paimpont (Car tour 5), just north of the N24 (Rennes to Ploërmel road). The picnic site is adjacent to the D40, beside the lake. *In addition to the lakeside scenery, the village of Paimpont boasts an old abbey, while Walks 17 and 18 are in the vicinity.*

19 TREHORENTEUC (Car tour 5; Walk 17; map page 114) ⊼

only accessible by car: no walking

🚗 Follow Car tour 5, or drive to Tréhorenteuc by leaving the D766 (Ploërmel to Dinan road) 10km north of Ploërmel: head for Néant-sur-Yvel, then take the D154 to Tréhorenteuc. Bear right through the village and pass an interesting old manor house. There is a visitors' car park and picnic area just beyond it. *This is a fairly secluded spot to break your journey. For those looking for a day out, the nearby forest offers several waymarked short walks.*

20 PLOUMANAC'H (Car tour 6; Walk 21; map pages 128-129; photograph pages 126-127)

only accessible by car: 10min on foot

🚗 Drive to Perros-Guirec (Car tour 6). Beyond the town the D788 goes north past La Clarté and, on reaching the coast, turns sharply southwest (by a viewing platform). Within 100m/yds take the minor road on the right, down to a car park. *Turn left to follow the coastal path until you come to the famed pink granite rocks; picnic anywhere between here and St-Guirec.*

21 TREBEURDEN (Car tour 6; touring map) ⊼

only accessible by car: no walking

🚗 Follow Car tour 6, or drive to Trébeurden: 1.6km/1mi north of the town, on the D788 corniche road, there is a picnic area and parking. *The site itself is nothing special, but the view, over a sea packed with red rocks and a myriad of islets, is spectacular. You may be tempted to drive out along the D21 and explore the Ile Grande in front of you.*

22 DINAN (Car tour 7; Walk 19; map pages 118-119; photographs pages 117, 121) ⊼

by bus/train: 1h10min on foot   by car: no walking or up to 1h10min

🚌 or 🚃 to Dinan. Follow the notes at the start of Walk 19, to get to the river Rance, but do not cross the bridge: turn left and follow the towpath northwards for just under an hour.

🚗 Drive to Dinan. Either park in the town and follow directions for bus and rail passengers above, or drive to a site with tables: head north on the D766, parallel with the railway. Take the first road on the right after you have left the town, and descend between wooded cliffs to the river. Turn left at the T-junction and, after 1.8km/1.1mi, turn right at cross-roads. Fork left in 250m/yds and then turn right in front of Taden's church. Follow the road down to the river, where you can park at the site. *The Rance is as wide as a lake here, with ducks, gulls and cormorants everywhere. It is a charming spot. For a short walk, turn left (as you face the river) and stroll along the towpath as far as the dam and lock gates. It will take you one hour there and back.*

❀ Touring

Brittany is an extensive holiday region. Even with seven car tours, I have had to omit several important centres. Those who would like to visit St-Malo and Dinard (and possibly the much-commercialised Mont St-Michel in Normandy) may do so by extending Tour 7 for an extra day. Most of the other significant places and buildings (indicated by a ★ in the notes and on the touring map) are visited. The notes are quite brief, concentrating on the 'logistics' of touring and on bringing you to the starting point for **walks** and **picnics**. Further information about the places visited can often be found in the text with the relevant walk.

The **roads** in Brittany are excellent. For rapid travel across the province there are the expressways, but these are unsuitable for sightseeing and, apart from brief stretches, I have avoided them. There are also many quite narrow country lanes. While these are well maintained, even with a large-scale map they can be very confusing, and it is all too easy to get lost. Where possible, I have avoided these as well. For ten months of the year you will have the roads almost to yourself but, in July and August, some, particularly near the coasts, will be very busy.

Unleaded **petrol** (*sans plomb*) is readily available, but at the time of publication not in all petrol stations. Sundays can occasionally be difficult for touring. *Many petrol stations do not open on Sundays.* It is also the day for **bicycle races**. The Bretons are fanatical cyclists, regularly closing off sections of road in the interests of safety. Sometimes the deviation signs will direct you back on to your original route. Sometimes the first deviation sign is the last you will see, leaving you lost on those country lanes. You have been warned!

Remember to **allow plenty of time for visits**. The times given are driving times, with no allowance for sightseeing. Distances quoted in the notes are *cumulative* from the departure point. They were measured in miles (for British motorists taking their own cars) and converted to kilometres, which will account for any slight discrepancies. A key to the **symbols** in the touring notes is on the touring map.

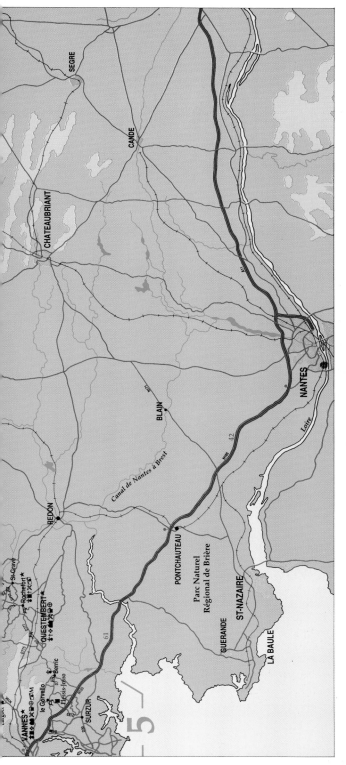

LEGEND/LEGENDE/LEGENDE/LÉGENDE

| 0 | 10km | 10 m | 20km |

● 17 —— motorway, distances/Autobahn, Kilometrierung
autoroute, distances

—— other roads/Fahrstraßen/autres routes

0-100 m (0-330 ft)

100-200 m (330-650 ft)

over/über/plus de 200 m (650 ft)

3 area of the car tour and number
Gebiet der Autotour mit zugehöriger Nummer
région et numéro de l'excursion en voiture

5 location of walk and number
Gebiet der Wanderung mit zugehöriger Nummer/
situation et numéro de la randonnée

🏨 ✗🍴 hotel, pension/Hotel, Gasthof/hôtel, auberge
restaurant/Restaurant/restaurant

⊕ 🏪 petrol station/Tankstelle/station-service
medical centre/Krankenhaus/centre de soins

♦ monastery, church or chapel/Kloster, Kirche oder
Kapelle/monastère, église ou chapelle

★ tourist attraction/touristische Sehenswürdigkeit
curiosité touristique

🎪 picnic tables/Picknickplatz mit Tischen
terrain de pique-nique

■ castle, fort/Burg, Festung/château, fort

π prehistoric site/prähistorische Stätte/site préhistorique

M museum/Museum/musée

+ [π] ❖ monument/Denkmal/monument
parish close/Pfarrbezirk/enclos paroissial
calvary/Calvaire/calvaire

📷 viewpoint/Aussichtspunkt/point de vue

WALKING MAPS/LANDKARTEN/CARTES DES RANDONNÉES

▭▭ sealed road/Fahrstraße/route goudronnée

══ lane or track/Weg, Schotterweg/chemin

⹁⹁ path or steps/Pfad oder Stufen/sentier

→⹁⹁ route of the main walk (green) with number
Wanderweg (grün) mit zugehöriger Nummer
itinéraire de la randonnée (vert) et numéro

┈┈ alternative route/Variante/variante

P picnic suggestion/Picknickvorschlag/suggestion de
pique-nique

🚌 bus stop/Bushaltestelle/arrêt des cars

🅿 car parking/Parkplatz/parking

Copyright © Sunflower Books

Morlaix • St-Thégonnec • Guimiliau • Landivisiau • Landerneau • Le Conquet • Lannilis • Le Folgoët • Château de Kerjean • St-Pol-de-Léon • Morlaix

242km/150mi; 6h driving

On route: Picnics (see pages 11-15) 1, 2, 3; Walk 1

The ancient kingdom of Léon in northwest Finistère is the least visited region in Brittany. Dominated by the great naval base and city of Brest (which the tour avoids), it boasts the most westerly coast of France. Rocky and wind-swept, it is pierced by long fiords, the Breton 'abers'. Here, too, are the most striking parish closes, the loftiest menhir, Brittany's finest 16th-century château, and the exquisite valley of the river Elorn.

The tour starts in **Morlaix** (✝▲▲✕⊕🖭MWC), after Brest the largest town in Léon. Leave the centre following signs for Quimper and, after 1.6km/1mi, go straight ahead at the crossroads for 'Quimper par CD712'. At 6km/4mi, cross first the railway and then the D785 (Quimper road), to make for St-Thégonnec. Some 3km/2mi further on follow 'Brest' and, at 11km/7mi, keep ahead at crossroads, to follow the D712 into **St-Thégonnec★** (13km/8mi ✝Ξ✝ ▲▲✕⊕), home to one of the most exciting of the parish closes (photograph page 50). Leave following signs for Landivisiau and Landerneau, still on the D712 (☍). At 16km/10mi turn left in the hamlet of **Kermat**, on the D31 to **Guimiliau★** (19km/12mi ✝Ξ✝✕), St-Thégonnec's great rival in the matter of parish closes, which boasts the most magnificent calvary in all Brittany. Both of these parishes are visited on Walk 1, and you can read more about them on pages 48-51. Turn right on the D111, pass to the left of the church, and follow signposting for Lampaul-Guimiliau (☍).

At 21km/13mi turn right at the roundabout for Lampaul and Landivisiau. When you enter **Lampaul★** (22km/14mi ✝Ξ✝▲▲✕☍), there is a picnic site and parking if you turn right just before the church, but the tour continues ahead, passing to the left of the church (noted for the richness of its decoration). Follow

Walk 5: the Nantes—Brest Canal

signposting for Landivisiau, on the D11, passing a picnic site (⊼) at 24km/15mi, beyond the railway tunnel.

Follow 'Centre Ville' into the busy town of **Landivisiau** (25km/16mi ♠♠✕⊕wc), then turn left for Landerneau. After 27km/17mi turn left at a roundabout for Landerneau, following the D712 along the valley of the river Elorn. You pass the picturesque Brézal Mill, opposite the ruined chapel of Pont-Christ, some 33km/21mi en route.

Make a short side-trip in **La Roche-Maurice** (38km/24mi ♠Ξ†), to see another exceptional parish close. Turn left to cross the Elorn, drive over the railway, and follow the twisting road up to the church. Look for the figure of Ankou ('Death') above the font on the outside of the 1640 ossuary. Return to the river and, beyond the bridge, turn left along the D712, to continue to Landerneau. Keep straight ahead in **Landerneau★** (43km/27mi ♠♠✕⬛⊕wc), beside the river, ignoring a street on the right signposted 'Brest par Guipavas', until you come to a roundabout at 45km/28mi. Ignore the first exit to the right ('Brest par N12'); keep straight ahead for 'Brest par Guipavas'.

Follow signs for Guipavas until you go under the railway (47km/29mi). On coming out of the tunnel, turn left uphill at once, on the D233 for La Forest-Landerneau. Still over-looking the Elorn (☎), pass through **La Forest-Landerneau** (50km/31mi) and carry on for Le Relecq. At 58km/36mi bear right on the D67 for **Guipavas**. Keep ahead at the roundabout when you get there but, at 60km/37mi, turn right at the T-junction with the D712. Take the first turn-

ing to the left (at traffic lights), joining the D67 for St-Renan and Goues-nou. Pass under the N12 expressway. At 64km/40mi, follow 'St-Renan' at the roundabout outside Gouesnou. At 66km/41mi turn left on the D67 for St-Renan and continue to follow similar signs for the next 11km/7mi. Go straight through **St-Renan** and, at 79km/49mi, turn right for

Car tour 5 and Walk 18: beside the river Aff

The Château de Costaérès, on the Pink Granite Coast (Car tour 6, Walk 21)

Plouarzel (D5). At 83km/52mi turn left on a minor road, signposted 'Menhir', and park 1.6km/1mi along. A path leads to the **Menhir de Kerloas** (🏛), the tallest menhir still standing in western Europe (11m/36ft). Returning to the car, turn right to carry on in the same direction as before, until you come to a T-junction (90km/56mi). Turn right. There is no sign, but this is the D67, and you are heading for Le Conquet. At 98km/61mi turn left on the C4, for Plougonvelin, keeping ahead at crossroads with the D789 some 3km/2mi along. Turn right at the roundabout in **Plougonvelin** for 'Pte de St-Mathieu'.

On reaching the **Pointe de St-Mathieu★** (106km/66mi 🖼❖), follow the D85 round to the right ('Le Conquet par a route touristique'). From **Le Conquet★** (111km/69mi ⚓🏔✕🖼) follow signs for Brest. Just beyond a picnic site 🪑P1) some 1.6km/1mi along, turn left on the D67 for Trébabu. After 0.5km/0.3mi turn left again, taking the D28 for Ploumoguer. Turn left in **Ploumoguer** (119km/74mi) for Plouarzel (still the D28; 🪑 after 1.6km/1mi). Beyond **Plouarzel** (122km/76mi) follow 'Brélès', keeping straight ahead at crossroads with the D5. Turn left at 129km/80mi and, at 130km/81mi, fork left on the D27, at the edge of Brélès (signposted 'Portsall par la côte' and 'Lanildut'). Beyond **Porspoder** (137km/85mi) continue to follow Portsall' (and also now 'Kersaint'; 🪑 after 3km/2mi). At

142km/88mi turn left on the C10 for 'Kersaint par la route touristique'. Pass through **Trémazan** (147km/91mi ☞❖), following signs 'Kersaint' and 'Ploudalmézeau', to join the D27. On your right are the ruins of Trémazan Castle (🏛), whither, some say, fled the lovers Tristan and Isolde.

From **Kersaint**, carry on to **Ploudalmézeau** on the D168, then follow 'Centre Ville'. At 151km/94mi turn left: follow signs for Lannilis, first on the D26, then on the D28. Some 3km/2mi along you reach the estuary of the Aber Benoît. There is a picnic site in **Tréglonou** shortly before you cross the Aber Benoît (161km/100mi ➋*P*2) and another one (➋) 1.6km/1mi further on, just as you enter **Lannilis**. Turn sharp left in the square (but be careful of *priorité à droite* here and throughout the village), to follow 'Lesneven', then bear right at the next junction. Stay on the D28 now, following 'Lesneven' for some 16km/10mi, until you reach the traffic lights in **Le Folgoët★** (179km/111mi ✝). Turn right, then left, to visit Jean de Montfort's impressive church, founded in thanksgiving for the victory at Auray (1364), which gained him the dukedom. Folgoët means 'Fool's Wood': at the time of the War of Succession there lived here a poor idiot named Salaün, who endlessly repeated the few words he knew: 'Lady Virgin Mary'. After his death a miracle occurred. There sprang from his grave (indeed, from his mouth!) a lily whose pistils formed the words 'Ave Maria'. Montfort built his church over the spring where Salaün used to drink.

Return to the traffic lights in Le Folgoët and turn right. (The tour continues now to St-Pol-de-Léon via Louis Barbier's magnificent 16th-century mansion, the finest in all Brittany, the Château de Kerjean. This necessitates a stop, since little can be seen from the road. If you do not have time for this, an alternative route to St-Pol is suggested at the end of the tour since, apart from Kerjean, the 40km/25mi stretch from here to

Car tour 4; Walk 13: Le Géant Menhir. See also photograph on page 96.

Car tour 7, Walk 19: picturesque Dinan; see also photograph page 117.

St-Pol is rather dull.) Having turned right at the traffic lights, after 1.6km/1mi, bear left on the D770 for **Lesneven**. Ignore a road on the right which leads to the German war cemetery but, beyond it, turn right (signposted 'St-Pol-de-Léon'). Continue to follow this signposting; you leave Lesneven on the D788. At 196km/122mi turn right on the D30 for **St-Vougay**, passing to the right of its church some 1.6km/1mi along. Then turn right, following 'Château de Kerjean' and, 1.6km/1mi further on, bear right again. You soon reach the entrance to the **Château de Kerjean**, on your right (🏛). On leaving Kerjean, turn left, and go left again on the D30 following 'St-Pol-de-Léon' and 'St-Vougay'. At 203km/126mi do not go back into St-Vougay, but fork right on the D229 for St-Pol-de-Léon. Some 1.6km/1mi along, turn right on the D788 through **Berven** (204km/127mi ✝Ξ): the parish close here is entered through a particularly fine triumphal arch.

At 219km/136mi follow 'St-Pol centre', and 'Toutes Directions' when you reach the town. **St-Pol-de-Léon★** (221km/137mi ✝⚠🏔✕🏪⊕WC) is a charming little town with many old houses and two wonderful buildings: the former cathedral and the Kreisker Chapel with its

Walk 3: a converted windmill near the hamlet of St-Norgard

magnificent spire soaring 77m/250ft into the air. Turn right in the town and follow 'Morlaix'; then bear left in front of a church, still following signposting for Morlaix. Leave St-Pol on the D769 for Morlaix and Carantec and, at 224km/139mi, turn right to join the D58 for Morlaix and Carantec. Cross the river Penzé and then turn left on the D173, signposted 'Carantec' and 'Morlaix par la corniche'. At 230km/143mi follow 'Morlaix par la corniche' again and, at 232km/144mi, turn right on the D73, passing a picnic site (*P*3) 3km/2mi along. Go through **Locquénolé**. Pass another picnic site () and turn left on the D769 () for Morlaix. Beyond **St-Martin-des-Champs** (240km/149mi) you re-enter **Morlaix** (242km/150m). Keep ahead towards the great railway viaduct ('Centre Ville'), or follow 'Quimper' to continue the tour, if you joined midway.

Alternative route from Le Folgoët to St-Pol-de-Léon

From the traffic lights in Le Folgoët, keep straight ahead on the D788, and do the same at the next lights, following 'Toutes Directions'. Turn left in **Lesneven** square for Brignogan, then twist through the rest of Lesneven following 'Brignogan', until you eventually leave town on the D770. At 188km/117mi keep straight ahead for 'Brignogan-Plages', to see a remarkable menhir. Fork left 5km/3mi further on, at the end of the road in **Brignogan-Plage**. Then turn left along the Rue du Menhir (signposted 'Plage du Phare et des Chardons Bleus'). The **Men Marz** ('Miracle Stone') menhir is soon reached (). It is 8m/26ft high and surmounted by a little cross. This was the Lan ar Paganis, or 'Land of the Pagans'; the inhabitants preferred their old religion to Christianity up until the 17th century ... and even then the missionaries had to 'Christianise' the menhir!

Returning to Brignogan, the one-way system takes you to 'Centre Ville' by a different route. Turn left at the crossroads, then bear right at the junction with the D770. Some 5km/3mi along turn left on the D10, heading for St-Pol. You pass through **Goulven** () and then **Plouescat** (211km/131mi), noted for its 17th-century covered market (or, to avoid the town centre, follow 'Toutes Directions' and 'Roscoff'). Continue along the D10, passing a picnic site () 5km/3mi beyond Plouescat. Drive through **Cléder** (217km/135mi) and, just before entering Sibiril, turn left. After 0.5km/0.3mi turn left again, to the 15th-century **Kérouzéré Castle** (). Return to **Sibiril**, turn left, and keep ahead at traffic lights 3km/2mi further on. Ahead you can see St-Pol's two towers: the cathedral and the Kreisker Chapel. At 229km/142mi follow 'St-Pol centre' at the roundabout; now pick up the main tour notes at the top of this page.

Ste-Marie-du-Ménez-Hom • Crozon • Camaret • Le
Faou • Daoulas • Ploudiry • Sizun • Commana •
Huelgoat • Brasparts • Pleyben • Châteaulin • Ste-Marie
246km/153mi; about 5h driving
On route: Picnics (see pages 12-13) 4-9; Walks 2-8

*The shoreline of the Crozon Peninsula, the valley of the river Aulne, the
Arrée Hills, and the Forest of Huelgoat comprise an area of such
exceptional beauty that it has been declared a regional natural park.
Besides its magnificent scenery, the region has many fine parish closes
and the two best dolmens in Finistère. The tour is circular, with no single
obvious starting place. I have used as its starting point the foot of Ménez-
Hom, for the benefit of motorists coming from Quimper and the south.
You should join it wherever is most convenient.*

Coming from the south on the D63 (the D47 beyond
Plomodiern), having followed signs for Châteaulin,
turn left for Crozon when you reach the D887 junction.
As you pass through the hamlet of **Ste-Marie** (♣†; photograph page 65; Walk 5) follow signs for Crozon and
Morgat. The tour begins at the foot of Ménez-Hom
(330m/1082ft; **P**8), on your right. Beyond some picnic
sites (14km/9mi and 18km/11mi ☞☶), you pass through
Tal-ar-Groaz (19km/12mi). Some 3km/2mi further on,
turn right in **Crozon** (23km14mi ♣▲✕🖳⊕) for Camaret and Morgat. The road to Morgat (**P**6 and Walk 3;
photograph pages 56-57) is passed, on the left, 6km/4mi
along. (Morgat, 'the pearl of the Crozon', is a pleasant
holiday town, not on the tour. If you have time, however,
it is well worth a detour.) The beach on your left 5km/3mi
beyond the Morgat turn-
off is the Anse de Dinan;
the rocks at the end of the
promontory are known
as 'Le Château de Dinan'.

Enter **Camaret** (34km/
21mi ♣▮❖▲△✕🖳⊕M
WC🚉**P**4), starting point
for Walk 2. Follow 'Pte
de Pen-Hir' and 'Port'. As
you drive along the port,
Vauban's Tower, shown
here, is on your right, at
the end of the mole. Turn
left at the end of the port
for the Pointe de Pen-Hir,

*Vauban's Tower
(Car tour 2 and Walk 2)*

The 16th-century 'triumphal arch' at Sizun; see also Walk 8.

passing a road on the right that leads to the beach of Pen-Hat (**P**5). Some 1.6km/1mi along you pass the rows of menhirs known as the **Alignements de Lagatjar**★ (37km/23mi 🏛). Keep ahead for the **Pointe de Pen-Hir**★ (38km/24mi 📷❖), which ends in a line of small islands called the **Tas de Pois** ('Heaps of Peas'). These are nesting grounds for numerous birds. Return along the same road but, just before reaching the *alignements*, turn right on the D8 for 'Crozon direct'. On leaving Camaret, turn left on the D355, signposted 'Pte des Espagnols'.

The **Pointe des Espagnols**★(📷), once a Spanish fort, affords wonderful views over the Brest roadstead. Follow the D355 south again, through **Roscanvel**, then bear left for Le Fret and Crozon. At 58km/36mi turn left on the D55 for Le Fret. In **Le Fret** (61km/38mi) turn right, cross the dam, then go left at the roundabout, for Lanvéoc, still on the D55. In **Lanvéoc** follow signs for Brest, keeping ahead at the roundabout (D63). From **Tal-ar-Groaz** follow signs for Le Faou and Brest, leaving to the left at the roundabout (D791). Ignore the turning to Landévennec 8km/5mi along; continue on the D791 to Le Faou. At 82km/51mi cross the Térénez suspension bridge over the river Aulne (📷), and follow 'Le Faou' through lovely scenery.

The ruins of the Abbey of Bon-Repos (Car tour 4, Walk 20); see also photograph page 125.

Turn left in **Le Faou** (♣▲▲�†) for 'Centre Ville', go over the bridge, and leave on the D770. At 95km/59mi bear left, following 'Quimper' but, as you approach the N165 expressway, do not turn right for Quimper: keep straight ahead for 'L'Hôpital-Ct' and drive northwest, parallel with the expressway. Pass through **L'Hôpital-Camfrout** and carry on for **Daoulas**★ (103km/64mi ♣Ξ†). Turn left at the traffic lights, following signs 'Abbaie' and 'Plougastel-Daoulas', but do not fail to stop to visit the abbey and parish close. The abbey was founded by Augustinian monks in the 12th century, but is now a Franciscan friary.

At 106km/66mi bear right for Loperhet. After 1.6km/1mi, go left at the next fork, then straight ahead at the crossroads. Drive through **Loperhet** on the D33, in the direction of Brest. At 114km/71mi turn right on the D29 for Landerneau, crossing the expressway. Follow 'Centre Ville' on entering **Landerneau**★ (124km/77mi ♣▲▲✕🍴 ⛁WC), then turn left to follow 'Toutes Directions' over the Elorn bridge. Beyond the bridge turn right for Sizun and, at the traffic lights, bear right on the D764, re-crossing the river, still following 'Sizun' (and now 'Huelgoat').

At 132km/82mi turn left on the C6. The parish close of **La Martyre** (♣Ξ†) is the oldest in Léon. Turn left in this village for Ploudiry (🅿 at 135km/84mi). Pass to the right of the church in **Ploudiry** (♣Ξ†) and look out for the figure of Ankou ('Death') on the ossuary wall, striking down representatives of all social classes. Bear right beyond the church. Ignore the first road on the right (to Roc'h Glaz) and continue along a country road to Sizun, bearing left at a fork some 1.6km/1mi along (Sizun is signposted here, as well as many farms and hamlets). Continue to follow signs for Sizun as far as the D764 junction, where you turn left (140km/87mi), passing 🅿 after 1.6km/1mi.

In **Sizun** (♣Ξ†▲▲⚐✕) stay on the D764 for Huelgoat and Carhaix. As you pass to the right of the church, notice the 16th-century lychgate (*arc de triomphe*) shown opposite, the finest in Brittany. It is from here that you set off on Walk 8. From Sizun the D764 takes you up into the Arrée Hills. At 153km/95mi turn left on the D211 into **Commana** (♣Ξ†⚐); bear right in the village centre, passing to the right of the church. At the D764 crossroads, go straight over and park in the car park on your right, to view one of the finest dolmens in Brittany, the **Allée Couverte du Mougau** (156km/97mi 🏛). Then return to the crossroads and turn right along the D764 for Huelgoat.

Pass **Roc'h Trévézel** (383m/1256ft 📷) on your right

after 161km/100mi and keep ahead at crossroads 1km further on for Huelgoat and Lorient. **Roc'h Trédudon**, at 387m/1269ft the highest point in Brittany, stands on your left. To your right is the **Yeun Elez** marshland (☎), now partially flooded. Follow the D764 southwards. Ignore the right turn for Brennilis, but take the next left turn (171km/106mi) for **Huelgoat★** (117km/110mi ☀†🏛▲✕☒ 🚐⊕☎wc**P7**), one of the prettiest places in Brittany and starting point for Walk 4 (photograph page 60).

Having driven beside the lake, turn right in the centre of Huelgoat on the D769a, for Pleyben and Quimper. At 179km/111mi keep straight ahead, ignore turnings to both Lorient and Morlaix, and cross over the D764. Descend to cross the river Elez and climb past **St-Herbot**. At 187km/116mi turn right on the D36 for **Brennilis** (☀†▲🏛). Away to your left is a nuclear power station. On the north side of the village, turn right for 100m/yds, following the sign 'Dolmen'. The **Ti ar Boudiked** ('Dwarf's House') is one of the largest dolmens, still partially encased in earth, as once they all were. Return to the D36 and turn right to continue north. At 193km/120mi turn left on the D764 again, in the direction of Morlaix. But after 1.6km/1mi turn left on the D42 for Botmeur and Brasparts; the road skirts the mysterious region of Yeun Elez. Having passed through the hamlet of **Botmeur**, turn left on the D785 for Brasparts (203km/126mi). Pass the D42 on your right after 2.4km/1.5mi: it leads to St-Rivoal, where Walks 6 and 7 begin. After 4.4km/2.7mi a lane on your right goes up to the chapel of St-Michel on the summit of **Ménez-Mikel★** (381m/1250ft; ☀☎**P9**; photograph page 74), another optional starting point for Walk 7.

On reaching **Brasparts** (214km/133mi ☀Ξ†), leave following signs for Pleyben, still on the D785 (🅿 at 217km/135mi and 219km/136mi). In **Pleyben** (224km, 139mi ☀Ξ†▲✕🚐) keep straight ahead across the square, to pass yet another outstanding parish close, where the calvary is combined with the triumphal arch. Some 1.6km/1mi along, turn right on the N164 for Châteaulin (🅿 after 3km/2mi). Cross the N165 expressway (232km/144mi) and carry on to Châteaulin on the D887. In **Châteaulin** (235km/146mi ☀▲△✕🚐⊕wc) follow 'Centre Ville', at the left of the river Aulne. Then make for Crozon and Morgat, crossing the river. Turn right, continue beside the river as far as the traffic lights, and then bear left for Crozon and Morgat, still on the D887. At 246km/153mi the D47, on your left, completes the circuit.

Quimper • Concarneau • Pont-Aven • Bénodet • Pont-Abbé • Penmarc'h • Pont-Croix • Audierne • Pointe du Raz • Confort • Douarnenez • Locronan • Quimper

253km/157mi; about 5h30min driving

On route: Picnics (see pages 11-15) 10,11; Walks 9-12

When the Romans left Britain in the 5th century, the people of Cornwall became the 'boat people' of their time, as they fled before the barbarians who now invaded the land. Migrants carry the names of their old homes with them, and so it was that Iaun Reith came to found a new Cornwall in southern Brittany. In the next century King Gradlon built Quimper to be the capital of Cornwall (spelt 'Cornouaille' by the French), and it is here that the tour begins.

Note: Throughout Finistère take care with *priorité à droite*. So many roundabouts now have signs saying that the *priorité* (right of way) has been changed, that it is easy to assume they all have. This is not the case and, where there is no warning sign, cars coming on to the roundabout will not give way to traffic already on it. The same is true of unmarked street junctions in the towns and villages. Cars coming from the right have right of way; and there are many such junctions. **Note also:** The D7-- roads were formerly N roads and will still be shown as such on older road signs.

Leave **Quimper★** (♣❖▲⚠✕🚽⊕📷MWC) or its ring road in the direction of Concarneau on the D783. After 7km/11mi turn right for **Concarneau★** (21km/13mi ⚠✕🚽⊕📷MWC), still on the D783. Follow 'Centre Ville' through this bustling fishing town, to arrive opposite the *ville close* (old town), built on an island and enclosed within Vauban's 17th-century walls. Leave Concarneau by heading in the direction of Quimperlé on the D322a, then turn right on the D783 and cross the river Moros. In **Trégunc** follow signs for Pont-Aven, still on the D783.

Pass a picnic site at 35km/22mi (🅿), then bear right to enter one of the prettiest of Breton towns, **Pont-Aven★** (37km/23mi ▲✕🚽⊕📷M), to this day a 'city of painters'. In former times corn was shipped on the tide to be ground in the mills here. The combination of river, port, mills, and mill-races created a picturesque setting that in 1865 attracted the attention of an American painter named Robert Wylie. Other American artists followed him, then English, French, and finally painters from all over Europe by the score. But it was in 1886 that history stepped into Pont-Aven in the person of Paul Gauguin, who took up residence in the auberge of Marie-Jeanne Gloanec, having quit Paris in search of that 'primitive and savage emotion' (and cheap living!) he would find five years later in Tahiti. With his friends and disciples Emile Bernard and Paul Sérusier, Gauguin developed in Pont-Aven a way of painting that many see as the start of modern art. In the century since then, the village has remained a Mecca for artists.* Explore the town (try to do at least *part* of Walk 12), then leave by the road on which you came in, bearing left to return to Concarneau, again on the D783. Having re-crossed the Moros (51km/32mi), avoid 'Centre Ville' and follow 'Quimper'. After 3km/2mi turn left for Quimper on the D783 in **Le Poteau Vert**. Do *not* take the D70 straight ahead (also signposted 'Quimper'): this would take you on to the N165 expressway ('Voie Rapide').

At 61km/38mi turn left for **La Forêt-Fouesnant** (♣Ξ† △✕) on the D44, to leave what has admittedly been a dreary road. After La Forêt continue on the D44 for Fouesnant and Bénodet. As you enter **Fouesnant** (66km/41mi ♣△▲✕�⊕WC), there is a picnic site on the right (☐). This district has the reputation of producing the only cider in Brittany to rival that of Normandy. Incidentally the distillate of cider in Brittany is not called *calvados* as in Normandy, but *eau-de-vie*.

Turn left at the T-junction for Bénodet, then right at the roundabout, all the time on the D44. In **Bénodet★** (74km/46mi ❖▲▲△✕➔⊕☐WC) turn left ('Bénodet Plage') if you want to visit this popular resort, or bear right on the D44 and follow signs for Pont-l'Abbé to continue the tour. Cross the river Odet (75km/47mi) and enter the country of the Bigouden, named after the traditional tall headgear of the women of the region, which even today you may occasionally see being worn as everyday dress.

At 81km/51mi pass on your right M Dussour's Museum of Mechanical Musical Instruments (**M**). After 1.6km/1mi turn left for **Pont-l'Abbé** (♣▲▲△✕➔⊕MWC), taking care with *priorité à droite*. At 85km/53mi turn right at the traffic lights for Loctudy and, at 92km/57mi, turn right on the D53, now following 'Penmarc'h'. Pass through **Plobannalec** and, at 103km/64mi, turn left on the D785 to enter **Penmarc'h★** (105km/65mi ♣❖♎▲△✕➔⊕☐MWC) Follow 'Penmarc'h centre', then 'Phare d'Eckmühl', and drive through the parishes of **Kérity** and **St-Pierre**, before coming to the great lighthouse (65m/213ft) that the Marquise de Blocqueville (née d'Eckmühl) gave to the

*If you read this book before leaving home, try to see reproductions of the following paintings before starting your holiday (your local library should have good works on the Post-Impressionists or modern art): Paul Sérusier: 'The Talisman'; Emile Bernard: 'Madeleine in the Bois d'Amour'; Paul Gauguin: 'Yellow Christ', 'Self-Portrait with Yellow Christ', and 'Green Christ'. See also notes for Walk 12.

nation in 1893. Now follow 'St-Guénolé, on the D80 (⊼),
and keep straight ahead in **St-Guénolé**, to pass to the right
of the port. Make a side trip by going ahead on the V11
'Rochers de St-Guénolé', to see the famous rocks (⊠);
afterwards, follow the road round to the left, past the port
and back to this point, where you will then turn right
'Musée Préhistorique'). Keep following signs for 'Musée'
and 'Pors Carn' until you reach the **Finistère Museum of
Prehistory** (113km/70mi **⏸**M*P*10). Walk 10 starts here,
and you will find notes on Torche Point and Notre-Dame
le Tronoën beginning on page 83.

At 114km/71mi turn left along the Rue de Câbles Sous-
Marins (the undersea cable link between France and
America comes ashore here), signposted 'Pointe de la
Torche'. Then turn left at first roundabout for 'Chapelle
le Tronoën'. After 1.6km/1mi turn left to visit the **Pointe
le la Torche** (**⏸**⊠; photograph page 82), or bear right
o continue the tour, still following signs for the 'Chapelle
le Tronoën' and turning left at the next two junctions.
Pass **Notre-Dame de Tronoën★** (119km/74mi **⏸**†✕) and
urn right. Keep right also at the fork, following the V5
owards St-Jean-Trolimon. At 122km/76mi bear right
signposted 'Pont-l'Abbé') but, soon, turn left in **St-Jean**
†), taking the D57 in the direction of Audierne and
Douarnenez. Enter **Plonéour-Lanvern** (129km/80mi); turn
eft on the D2 for Audierne, going through **Pouldreuzic**
and **Plozévet** (†▲△). At 145km/90mi turn left on the
D784 but, 5km/3mi further on, fork right on the D2 into
Pont-Croix (†△). The 67m/220ft-high church steeple here,
built in 1450, was to provide the model for the twin spires
of Quimper's cathedral four hundred years later. Turn left
n Pont-Croix on the D765, following 'Audierne'. Pass an
attractively-located picnic area (⊼*P*11) and then enter
Audierne (158km/98mi **†▲✕➾⊕**), another busy fishing
port. Follow 'Centre Ville', and turn right at the end of the
harbour, following 'Plogoff' and 'Pte du Raz' on the D784.

At 164km/102mi turn left down a minor road, by a
signpost '1km à **Chapelle St-Tugen**' (†WC). St Tugen stands
on the right of the sanctuary, holding a key and accom-
panied by a mad dog, for he is the protector against mad
dogs and rabies. From the chapel turn right on the V2
and, at 166km/103mi, bear left for 'Pointe du Raz' and
Le Loc'h'. Soon bear right in **Primelin**, pass the church,
and turn left, following signs as before. After driving
through **Le Loc'h**, turn left on the D784 (169km/105mi).
Pass through **Plogoff**, and continue to the **Pointe du Raz★**

(177km/110mi ❖🔺△✕📷WC), where there is pay parking. This striking, if over-popular headland is the starting point for Walk 11.

Turn round and, 0.8km/0.5mi along, bear left on the V8 (signposted 'Douarnenez' and 'Baie des Trépassés'). Beyond the **Baie des Trépassés**, follow the road (D607) to the right for Douarnenez, turning right on the D7 after 1.6km/1mi. At 190km/118mi pass a road on the left to the Cap Sizun Bird Sanctuary. Go through **Beuzec** (196km/122mi) and, 5km/3mi further on, turn right on the D302 to Confort, shortly forking left. At 204km/127mi turn left ('Douarnenez') and enter **Confort** (🔺†) on the D765 (in spite of sign claiming it is N165). Inside the church there is a unique 400-year-old carillon wheel: dumb or speech-handicapped children have been brought here for centuries, to ring the bells. It is claimed that throughout the church's history there have been miracle cures.

Soon after passing the D43 to Pouldergat (on the right), take the next minor road, on the left (208km/129mi): it is signposted 'Chapelle de Kérinec'. In 1.6km/1mi turn left at crossroads for the church of **Notre-Dame de Kérinec** (🔺), yet another fine example of ecclesiastical architecture. From the church return to the crossroads and keep straight ahead. Turn left at the next T-junction, and then go right at the first turning (signposted 'St-They'; 213km/132mi). After 1.6km/1mi pass the road leading to St They's chapel on your right. At 214km/133mi turn right and follow the C10 into **Douarnenez** (217km/135mi 🔺🔺△✕🔌⊕📷 WC), one of the busiest of the Breton ports. The island in the bay, named after Tristan, was the lair of Brittany's most feared brigand, La Fontenelle, who terrorised the region in the 16th century. Turn left and follow 'Autres Directions' into the town, thereafter following 'Locronan' or 'Châteaulin'. At 219km/136mi join the D7 at a T-junction and continue to follow signs for Locronan.

On reaching **Locronan** ★ (227km/141mi 🔺🔺△✕WC) park in car park and walk into this picturesque village, from where Walk 9 follows in part the route of the famous pilgrimage of the Grande Troménie. After your visit, return to the roundabout, follow 'Toutes Directions', and then head for Quimper on the D63. Pass by Plogonnec and, at 232km/144mi, fork right for **Le Croëzou**, still on the D63, a far quieter and prettier road than the D39. Follow signs into **Quimper** (243km/151mi), making for 'Centre Ville' at the roundabout and then 'Toutes Directions' and 'Concarneau' to continue the tour, if you joined midway.

Auray • Ste-Anne-d'Auray • Baud • St-Nicolas-des-Eaux
• Pontivy • Mur-de-Bretagne • Le Faouët • Quimperlé
• Hennebont • Carnac • Locmariaquer • Auray

272km/169mi; 6h driving
On route: Picnics (see pages 11-15): 12-16, Walks 13, 15, 16, 20
Western Morbihan parades before us all that is most characteristic of Brittany: ancient towns, fine churches and abbeys, gorgeous river valleys, forests, that eerie inland sea whence it takes its name, and some of the most famous megalithic remains in the world, including the Alignments of Carnac.

The tour starts at the ancient town of **Auray**★ (♣✢▲✕➤⊕☞WC), near the Gulf of Morbihan. Leave to the north, along Avenue Foch and the D768, in the direction of Baud and Pontivy. Some 2.5km/1.5mi from the town centre, turn left for the **Abbaye de la Chartreuse**, a Carthusian monastery from 1482 to 1790. It was built around a chapel raised by Jean de Montfort, on the site of his victory over Charles du Blois and Duguesclin that ended the Breton War of Succession in 1364. Leaving the abbey, turn round, cross the D786, and take the D120 opposite for Ste-Anne-d'Auray. On your right is the Champ des Martyrs: In June 1795 a small army of French Royalist exiles was put ashore from British ships at Carnac in the Bay of Quiberon, to join those Breton anti-Republican rebels who were known as Chouans. The uprising was put down, and many of the captured rebels were shot in this field. Their remains were later carried to the Abbaye de la Chartreuse.

At 5km/3mi, having crossed the river Loc'h, turn right for **Ste-Anne-d'Auray**★ (6km/4mi ♣✢△M), the most important place of pilgrimage in all Brittany. Here, too, is the National Cemetery and a memorial to the 250,000 Bretons who died in the First World War — one in fourteen of the entire population, a proportion unequalled among the other combatants and, perhaps, in any war ever. Keep ahead at the crossroads, passing the basilica, and leave on the D17, soon turning left for Plumergat. In **Plumergat** follow 'Locminé' but, after 3.5km/2mi, turn left at the **Le Poteau** crossroads for Baud (D779). Some 5km/3mi along, continue to follow 'Baud' at crossroads, and pass through **Bieuzy**. Turn right in **Camors** (27km/17mi) on the D768, still following 'Baud' (⌷ 3km/2mi along).

In **Baud** (33km/21mi ♣✢▲△✕➤⊕) turn left on the D724 (signposted 'Languidic' and 'Hennebont') and, after 1km/0.5mi, turn left again, for '**Vénus de Quinipily**'. Park on the right, pay at the gatehouse, and go through the garden to see the famous Roman(?) idol, possibly of the goddess Isis, once the object of 'impure rites'. Drive back up the road and turn right. In only a few metres, turn left up the first lane (next to a house and signposted 'Manete lann'), and go through a farm. Keep straight ahead at the crossroads, following this narrow lane as it twists round another farm and continues beside the N24 expressway. At 37km/23mi turn left on the D142 (signposted 'Melrand' and go under the expressway; then carry straight on. Pass through **St-Barthélemy** (42km/26mi) and the hamlet of **St-Thuriau**, then cross the railway and river Blavet.

At 48km/30mi fork right on the D156 for **Bieuzy** (♦). From there keep ahead, following 'St-Nicolas-des-Eaux' and 'Pontivy' for 5km/3mi. Turn right for St-Nicolas on the R3 and drop down to the Blavet, doubling back to drive beside the river. Pass a picnic area (♠P12) and enter the village of **St-Nicolas-des-Eaux★** (63km/39mi ♦✿▲ △✕🕿). Turn left and cross the river, then drive up the hill opposite on the D1. After 1.6km/1mi fork left, for Talvern-Nénez and 'Chapelle de St-Nicodème'. On reaching the 16th-century chapel (you saw its massive tower and steeple from across the river), keep straight ahead on the winding road for another 2km/1.2mi; then, at the D768 junction, turn left for Pontivy. Drive straight through **Pontivy** (77km/48mi ♦✿▲✕🗩⊕🚻WC; Walk 16), following 'Autres Directions' initially, then bearing left on the D767 for Mur-de-Bretagne.

Bypass Neulliac and, on leaving **Mur-de-Bretagne** (93km/58mi ♦▲△✕🗩⊕🕿), head for Rostrenen. After 1.6km/1mi turn left on the N164, beside Guerlédan Lake: its dam now effectively blocks the Nantes-Brest Canal (shown on page 17). After 6km/4mi there are fine views over the lake (🕿♠P13) and, 3km/2mi further on, you come to **Bon-Repos Abbey★** (✿M P15; photographs pages 24 and 125). Walk 20 begins here. Turn right now, up the D44, signposted 'Corlay' and 'Circuit Touristique' through the **Gorges du Daoulas** (🕿). At 109km/68mi turn left in **Laniscat** (signposted 'St-Nicolas, Corlay, Uzel'). Bear left again in front of the church, following 'Gouarec' and left once more at the next junction (D76), still following 'Gouarec'. In **Le Poteau** (114km/71mi) the road number changes to D5. Enter **Gouarec** and turn right for Rostrenen on the N164 (♠ after 5km/3mi).

Turn left in **Rostrenen** (126km/78mi ♦) on the D790 for Plouray and Quimperlé. After 14km/9mi keep straight ahead at the crossroads in **Plouray**, still on the D790, and following 'Le Faouët' and 'Quimperlé'. You pass to the left of the church. Go straight over at the large crossroads outside the village; 1.6km/1mi along, you will see a sign for the **Abbaye de Langonnet**. Bear left after 3km/2mi, following 'Abbaie', then turn right to visit the abbey, where the 13th-century chapel (once the chapterhouse) is the oldest part now remaining. Today the abbey is a rest home for retired priests and houses a small museum devoted to African missions. Return to the road and continue towards Le Faouët along the valley of the river Ellé (photograph pages 102-103). Keep left at a fork 1.6km/1mi along. At 156km/97mi keep ahead at the D769 crossroads for Le Faouët and Quimperlé then, almost at once, turn left.

If you wish to detour to the Chapelle de Ste-Barbe (Walk 15), take the next turning left, then return to this point and follow 'Centre Ville' into **Le Faouët★** (158km/98mi ♣❖▲▲△✕➾⊕☜WC). Walk 15 starts here and visits the chapels of Ste-Barbe and St-Fiacre. On reaching the square, which boasts a 16th-century covered market, turn right, following 'Scaër, Quimperlé, St-Fiacre'. After 1.6km/1mi bear left to the chapel of St-Fiacre (*P*14), then continue along the D790 for another 17km/11mi.

Enter **Quimperlé★** (179km/111mi ♣▲▲△✕➾⊕MWC), at the confluence (*kemper* in Breton) of the rivers Ellé and Isole. It has some interesting old houses (including the 'Archers' House', now a museum), and the church of Sainte-Croix, built in the Middle Ages to emulate the Holy Sepulchre in Jerusalem. Turn left to leave, following 'Lorient' and 'Pont Scorff'.

At 184km/114mi leave the Lorient road, turning left on the D62 for Pont-Scorff. After 9km/6mi keep straight ahead in **Pont-Scorff** for Hennebont on the D26, crossing the river Scorff. Go under the D18 and, on entering **Hennebont** (206km/128mi ♣❖▲▲△✕➾⊕WC), cross the river Blavet and turn right ('Toutes Directions'). Hennebont is another town with a splendid steeple (65m/213ft) and the remains of former ramparts. It also has one of the largest stud farms in France, with some 140 stallions. Keep the river on your right and, as you leave the town, go under the railway viaduct and turn left on the D9 for Kervignac. In **Kervignac** (214km/133mi ♣) keep ahead for Carnac and Quiberon; then, some 1.6km/1mi further on, keep straight ahead into **Merlevenez** (217km/135mi ♣). At the crossroads in the village keep ahead for Carnac, passing to the right of the church with its Romanesque doorway, one of very few remaining in Brittany.

On rejoining the D9 after 1.6km/1mi, turn right. A 224km/139mi, at the junction with the D781, bear lef for Carnac and Quiberon, soon crossing the estuary o the Etel at **Belz**. From now on the route is bordered by megaliths, for this is the centre of a great pre-Gallic culture its dominant feature being a highly-developed cult of the dead. At 237km/147mi you come to a road junction and follow signs for **Carnac**★ (240km/149mi ♠🏋✣🏔▲△✕ ☕⊕🐚🗛Mwc). Just as you reach the town, turn left (sign posted 'Auray' and '**Alignements**'). Soon you will drive beside some of the most famous pre-historic monuments in the world: thousands of upright stones arranged in parallel lines. Walk 13 would take you amongst them see photographs on pages 20 and 96. Follow the menhirs for some 3km/2mi in the direction of Auray, then turn right on the D186 for La Trinité-sur-Mer. Turn left at the T-junction in **La Trinité** (246km/153mi 🏔△✕☕WC) then bear left round the port, following 'Locmariaquer and 'Auray par Crac'h'.

Now on the D781, swing right, round the bay. Cros the river Crac'h (🚗) and, at the traffic lights, follow 'Locmariaquer'. After 1.6km/1mi keep straight ahead a the crossroads, bear right at the junction at **Le Chat Noir** and enter **Locmariaquer**★ (256km/159mi ♠🏋✣🏔△✕ ☕⊕🐚WC). Signs (on your right) will direct you to its mos important archaeological features. One is the **Grand Menhir**. It is now in pieces but, before it was struck by lightning in the 18th century, it was the largest of them all (20.3m/67ft). The other is the **Table des Marchand** ('Merchants' Table'), one of the most impressive dolmens Carry on to park by the harbour, for a magnificent view over the Gulf of Morbihan, then follow 'Plages' to ar attractive picnic area (258km/160mi 🍴*P*16). Drive bacl

along the D781 as far as the junction at Le Chat Noir (264km/164mi), then turn righ on the D28 for Auray. Or entering **Auray** (272km/169mi) those wishing to continue the tour to a different starting poin should turn left in the centre along Avenue Foch and leave or the D768 for Baud and Pontivy.

Well at the Chapelle de Ste-Barbe (Walk 15), near Le Faouët

Vannes • St-Gildas-de-Rhuys • Questembert •
Rochefort-en-Terre • Malestroit • Paimpont • Ploërmel
• Josselin • Guéhenno • Trédion • Elven • Vannes

*266km/165mi; 6h driving. The tour can be shortened by 53km/33mi
by omitting the circular section from Ploërmel to Paimpont.*

On route: Picnics (see pages 11-15) 17-19; Walks 14, 17, 18

*Whether it be the mysterious inland sea of Morbihan, picturesque villages
like Rochefort-en-Terre, the mediaeval castles of Sucinio and Josselin,
Merlin's enchanted forest of Brocéliande, the parish close of Guéhenno,
or Kerguehennec Park's open-air display of modern sculpture, this tour
has much to entrance you.*

The tour starts at **Vannes★** (★👫❖✕🚇⊕🏠MWC) on the
Gulf of Morbihan, the first capital of Brittany. Leave
the city following 'Nantes'. Continue on the D779 and
join the N165. Leave at the next exit, for Sarzeau (D780;
5km/3mi). To your right is the Gulf of Morbihan ('Ar mor
bihan' is Breton for 'the little sea'). At 17km/11mi turn left
and follow signs for the **Château de Sucinio**. Some
3km/2mi along, turn left on the D198; then bear right
almost at once, following the same signposting, to arrive
at the ruins of this imposing 13th-century castle (👫), once
the summer home of the Dukes of Brittany.

Drive back to the D198 junction and turn left. This time
keep straight ahead (signposted 'Vannes/Itinéraire con-
seillé'). At 24km/15mi turn right following signs 'Sarzeau'
and 'St-Gildas'; then, 1.6km/1mi further on, turn left for
St-Gildas. Continue following 'St-Gildas' at the roundabout. The parish church of **St-Gildas-de-Rhuys** (32km/
20mi ★▲▲△✕) was once the chapel of an abbey, founded
in the 6th century by St Gildas (his tomb is behind the
high altar, his arms and legs in the treasury). The philo-
sopher monk Abélard presided over it for an utterly-
miserable decade (as he described in his letters to his
beloved Héloïse). The monks were a lawless lot, who
hated Abélard for trying to discipline them. Eventually
they plotted to kill him. In fear for his life, he fled the
abbey in 1132.

On leaving St-Gildas, turn left on the D198 for Arzon,
to reach the junction with the D780 (39km/24mi). Turn
left again and continue towards Arzon for 2.3km/1.4mi,
then park in the roadside car park. Walk up the gravel
track on your right for 200m/yds to the Tumiac Tumulus.
From its summit (34m/112ft 🏠) you can experience the
view of the Gulf of Morbihan and Quiberon Bay that Julius
Caesar enjoyed from this hill in 56BC, as he watched the
Roman fleet commanded by Brutus vanquish the navy of

the native Veneti and so gain Armor for Rome. (However, some geologists maintain that the Gulf had not yet been formed …)

Return to the car park and drive back along the D780, following 'Vannes'. Some 13km/8mi along turn right on the D20 for Surzur, turning left into the village after 6km/4mi. Leave **Surzur** on the D183, following 'Le Gorvello'. At 66km/41mi cross the N165 and follow signs for the Château de Plessis. After 3km/2mi turn right for a brief side-trip to the **Château de Plessis-Josso** (🏛), then return and continue (🎋) into the attractive village of **Le Gorvello**. Here bear right on the D7 for Questembert. Some 5km/3mi along, turn left at the D140 junction and continue on the D7 for Questembert, via **Berric** (🎋). After 1.6km/1mi notice the 15th-century chapel of Our Lady of Virtue, on your left. Keep right 6km/4mi further on, to enter **Questembert** (84km/52mi ✚†❖🔺✕🖵⊕WC), with its sturdy market hall dating from 1675.

Leave on the D7 for Rochefort-en-Terre, passing two picnic areas (🎋 3km/2mi, 9km/6mi). Note that after crossing the D775 your road number changes to D777. Follow signs into the village of **Rochefort-en-Terre** (93km/58mi ✚†🔳✕👜WC), all roses and geraniums and gorgeous stone houses. Leave Rochefort on the D774, making for St-Gravé, then fork right at the bottom of the valley, to continue on the D777 (🎋 at 95km/59mi). Just on the approach to St-Gravé, look for a road that forks back to the left (not signposted). Turn down this road, the D764, which takes you into the valley of the river Oust and on to **Malestroit** (116km/72mi ✚🔺△✕🖵). Turn right for Ploërmel on the D764 (🎋 3km/2mi along) and, at 124km/77mi, turn right on the N166 for Ploërmel.

If you intend to omit the circular drive round the forest of Paimpont (as mentioned at the beginning of the touring notes) either follow 'Centre Ville' into Ploërmel, to visit the town, or turn left for Josselin on the N24. The main tour circles the forest: turn right on the N24, in the direction of Rennes. After 6km/4mi pass through **Campénéac** (139km/86mi) and then turn left on the D312 (140km/87mi) for Paimpont. Pass the **Château de Trécesson** (🏛) 1.6km/1mi along. On your right are the military training grounds of the Camp de Coëtquidan. Continue following signs for Paimpont. Beyond the hamlet of **Le Châtenay** (Walk 18; photograph page 18) the road is numbered D40. In **Paimpont★** (150km/94mi ✚🔺△✕🖵⊕👜WC) turn left at the roundabout, following 'Centre Bourg'. The picnic area on the left overlooking the mere (⊼P18) is a splendid setting. There was an abbey here from the 12th century until the Revolution, when the village replaced it. The chapel is now the parish church, and the abbey buildings house the town hall. Turn right just before reaching the abbey, pass through the gateway, turn left, and keep straight ahead on the D773. At 158km/98mi turn left on the D2, signposted 'Mauron' and 'Concoret'. Some 1.6km/1mi along, turn left by **Concoret** church for Tréhorenteuc, and soon bear left again. At 164km/102mi follow 'Tréhorenteuc D141' straight ahead at the crossroads. Then, 1.6km/1mi further on, turn left, following similar signposting. You pass a road off to the left 1.6km/1mi along, signposted 'Camping de Barenton'; it leads to the hamlet of Folle Pensée and the Fountain of Barenton, linked with the wizard Merlin.

Turn left on entering the tiny village of **Tréhorenteuc** (171km/106mi ♣) and follow 'Ploërmel', still on the D141. Pass a charming old manor house and, on leaving the village, bear right. You pass the starting point for Walk 17 (⊼P19), through the alarmingly-named 'Valley of No Return'. Continue to follow signs for Ploërmel and, after 9km/6mi, turn left at the ring road. At 179km/111mi turn right at the roundabout for 'Centre Ville', coming into **Ploërmel** (185km/115mi ♣✣▲▲✕➿⊕Mwc).

Leave Ploërmel following signs for Josselin. Some 6km/4mi along the N24, look out for the obelisk (✣) set amid trees between the carriageways on your left. This is La Pyramide, site of the 'Combat des Trente' where, in March 1351, Jean de Beaumanoir and thirty of his Breton knights from Josselin Castle engaged Richard Bemborough and thirty mainly English knights from Ploërmel in man-to-man combat. The Bretons won, and their names are written on the obelisk. (Behind the obelisk there is also a far older monument to the battle.) The English dead lie buried in the nearby 'Champ des Anglais'. At the end of this exhausting day, when the wounded Beaumanoir asked for water, Geoffroy du Bois gave his famous reply, 'Drink thy blood, Beaumanoir, 'twill quench thy thirst.'

In 3km/2mi turn off the N24 for **Josselin★** (196km/ 122mi ♣■✣▲▲✕➿⊕🚗Mwc), where Walk 14 begins and ends. Only the outer wall remains of the Rohans' impressive mediaeval castle (⊼P17), for the house itself was largely rebuilt in the 19th century. In addition to the castle, Josselin has a fine church (the tower may be climbed), some interesting old houses, and a museum in which the Rohan collection of 600 antique dolls is displayed. Leave Josselin following signs for Locminé and rejoin the N24. At 204km/127mi turn left on the D778 for Vannes and Guéhenno. **Guéhenno** (209km/130mi ♣☰†🔺WC) is noteworthy for its parish close. The 1550 calvary was vandalised during the Revolution, but restored in 1853. Unable to afford the charges of the local masons, the parish priest and his curate set about recarving the heads themselves.

Follow 'Vannes' out of the village and soon turn right on the D123 for Bignan. At 214km/133mi cross the D155. Bear left at a T-junction 1.6km/1mi beyond that junction and, at 217km/135mi, turn left at the junction with the D11. (If you go straight over, after 1.6km/1mi you will come to the entrance to the Domaine de Kerguehennec, a sculpture park where a splendid collection of modern works is being assembled. If you take this detour, return to this point afterwards, to continue the main tour.)

Some 5km/3mi beyond the junction with the D11, turn left on the D1 and drive into **St-Jean-Brévelay** (224km/ 139mi ♣🔺✕). Follow the road round to the left, then continue straight ahead, to head due east on the D778 for Plumelec. (Do *not* follow the road round to the right for Vannes.) After 3km/2mi fork right on the D1, following 'Plumelec' and 'Elven'. Turn right beyond the church in **Plumelec** (233km/144mi ♣†🔺) and continue on the D1 towards Elven.

Cross the river Claie after 3km/2mi and, at 239km/ 148mi, enter **Trédion** (🔳❖🏛🎋), where roadside picnic tables enjoy a fine view of the château shown on the cover. Carry on along the D1 and, after 6km/4mi, enter **Elven**. Turn right for Vannes and follow signs 'Fortresse de Largoët'. Leave on the D1, following 'Vannes' and 'Le Tours d'Elven'. Join the N166 and immediately turn right for the **Fortresse de Largoët** ('Towers of Elven' 🔳). It was home to the Malestroit family, whose guest from 1474 to 1476 was Henry Tudor, one day to be King Henry VII of England. It was destroyed by Charles VIII, when his troops invaded Brittany in 1488.

From the ruined castle return to the N166 and continue towards Vannes, forking right after 11km/7mi and soon re-entering **Vannes** (263km/163mi). Vannes takes its name from the Veneti who first lived here. It has much to interest the tourist, particularly in the Old Town. Follow 'Centre Ville' and 'Port' to see the town, or 'Nantes' to continue the tour, if you joined midway.

6 COTES-D'ARMOR

Lannion • Guincamp • Quintin • Kermaria • Paimpol • Pointe de l'Arcouest • Tréguier • Perros-Guirec • Ploumanac'h • Trégastel-Plage • Trébeurden • Lannion

253km/157mi; 6h30min driving

On route: Picnics (see pages 11-15) 20, 21; Walk 21

Côtes-d'Armor possesses some attractive inland countryside, not least the lovely valley of the river Trieux. It has many places and buildings of great interest, for example: the castle of Tonquédec, the chapels of Kerfons and Kermaria-an-Iskuit, and Beauport Abbey. Nonetheless, when your holiday is over, what you will remember most vividly will be the Breton Corniche beside the incredible Pink Granite Coast.

Lannion (✝🏠✕🚌⊕WC), close to several of the holiday resorts of the north coast, has been chosen as the start of the tour. On entering the town, follow 'Toutes Directions' initially, and then 'Autres Directions'. When you see Ploubezre signposted, leave Lannion to the south, on the D11, entering **Ploubezre** after 3km/2mi. At 5km/3mi fork left beside a wayside calvary (signposted 'Chapelle de Kerfons'). Bear left 1.6km/1mi further on. The road surface is a little rough until you reach the chapel (8km/5mi ✝). It is normally open during July and August, to enable you to admire the 15th-century carved rood-screen. Return to the D11 (remember to turn right after 1.6km/1mi at the T-junction), where you now turn left. After 3km/2mi turn left again, to view the Château de Kergrist (🏚; signposted), built in the 14th and 15th centuries. Again return to the D11 and turn left.

At 17km/11mi turn left along the D30 for Pluzunet. Cross the river Léguer and, at 23km/14mi, turn left on the D31 for the Château de Tonquédec. In little over 1.6km/1mi, turn left in **Tonquédec**, following the sign for the château, then turn right on the D31b beyond the church. The castle (26km/16mi 🏚📷), which was first built in the 13th century and rebuilt in the 15th century, was finally destroyed on Cardinal Richelieu's orders in 1622. There is a superb view from its walls.

Return to Tonquédec and follow the D31 (signposted 'Bégard') back to its junction with the D30. Here turn left to continue via **Pluzunet** to **Bégard** (39km/24mi). Turn right at the crossroads (avoiding 'Centre Ville'), then go right again on the D15 for Louargat and Belle-Isle. As you approach Louargat, the hill to your left is Ménez-Bré. Turn right on the D712 in **Louargat**, following 'Belle-Isle'. After 3km/2mi turn left for Belle-Isle on the D712, and cross the N12 expressway. Coming into Belle-Isle over the bridge, look out for the narrow D22 turning sharply to the left. You will take this road after visiting the village. **Belle-Isle-en-Terre** (52km/32mi) takes its name from the confluence of the rivers Guic and Léguer.

Leave Belle-Isle following 'Guincamp N12' and, just before the bridge, fork right down the D22, your immediate destination being Gurunhuel. At 55km/34mi bear right at a fork and, at 56km/35mi, keep ahead at crossroads, on a fairly wide road. At 58km/36mi ignore a minor road on the left. At 60km/37mi fork right into **Gurunhuel** (63km/39mi ⚬†), still on the D22. Do pause to inspect the 16th-century calvary, if only to observe the souls of the two robbers leaving their bodies and being received by an angel and a demon respectively. Turn left on leaving, and take the D20 to **Guincamp** (77km/48mi ⚬▲✕⚏⊕), where you follow 'Centre Ville'.

Leave via the Rue Ruello and the D767 for Corlay. (Or you may find it easier to follow 'St-Brieuc' as far as the N12 expressway, then get on the expressway in the direction of Morlaix, and leave it again at the next exit.) Follow the D767, one of the most beautiful roads in Brittany, south from Guincamp for 27km/17mi, along the valley of the river Trieux. At **La Clarté** (105km/65mi) turn left for Le Vieux Bourg and Quintin. After 3km/2mi notice the fairly unusual Christianised menhir bearing a cross. At 113km/70mi turn right in **Le Vieux Bourg** for St-Bihy (D63), passing to the right of the church. After 3km/2mi fork right. Pass to the right of the church in **St-Bihy** and keep straight ahead. Some 1.6km/1mi further on fork left on the C1 for Quintin. After 119km/74mi turn left at the junction with the D790 and follow it into **Quintin** (122km/76mi ⚬▮▲✕⚏⊕).

Turn left at the traffic lights and head for Châtelaudren on the D7 (🛱 at 132km/82mi). Go under the expressway and enter **Châtelaudren** (140km/87mi ⚬). Turn left, then right, following 'Lanvollon', still on the D7. Pass through **Tressignaux** and **Lanvollon** (151km/94mi). Turn left at the T-junction, on the D6, then keep ahead at the traffic lights. Pass to the left of the church and bear right on the D79 for Pléhédel and Pludal. At 153km/95mi keep ahead at crossroads and, at 156km/97mi, fork right on the D94 and enter **Pludal**. Go over the crossroads and pass to the left of the church, keeping ahead on the D94 for Lanloup.

On leaving Pludal, fork left. At 159km/99mi turn left at crossroads with the D21 (signposted 'Chapelle Kermaria 0,2km'), to arrive at the church of **Kermaria-an-Iskuit** (⚬), famous for its 15th-century frescoes (the 'Dance of Death').

Notice, too, the balcony from which the local *seigneur* dispensed justice. Return to the crossroads and turn left. Keep straight ahead for 3km/2mi, then turn left for Paimpol at the junction with the D786. At 172km/107mi pass the ruins of **Beauport Abbey** on the right, founded in the 13th century by the White Canons. Turn right at the roundabout in **Paimpol** (175km/109mi ✣🄰△✕🖳⊕Mwc), for 'Centre Ville' and 'Port'. Drive round the harbour and turn left on the D789, following 'l'Arcouest' (🝙 at 177km/110mi). Go through **Ploubazlanec** and follow signs for the **Pointe de l'Arcouest**★ (182km/113mi ✣🖝).

Return to Ploubazlanec (be careful of the one way system) and go back to Paimpol. At 187km/116mi take the first exit off the roundabout, for Tréguier. Drive round the church and follow 'Tréguier' and 'Lannion' on the D786, crossing the river Trieux and passing some picnic areas (🝙 193km/120mi, 200km/124mi). Beyond the river Jaudy you enter **Tréguier** (201km/125mi ✝✣🄰✕🖳⊕ Mwc). Tréguier has two famous sons. One is St-Yves, the 13th-century lawyer who was canonized in 1347 for his incorruptibility and readiness to represent the poor. You will see his tomb in the town's magnificent cathedral. The other famous son is Ernest Renan (1823-92), the 'modernist' Catholic writer whose 'Life of Christ' scandalised orthodox Catholics.

To continue the tour, keep left beyond the bridge for Lannion and Perros-Guirec. At 208km/129mi turn right at the roundabout onto the D6 for Perros-Guirec. Some 13km/8mi further on, turn right again at the roundabout in **Perros-Guirec**★ (✝🄰△✕🖳⊕🖝wc) and drive round the port. At 222km/138mi fork right to follow a road signposted 'N786d' (actually the D788) around the coast. Pass a viewing platform after 1.6km/1mi (🖝*P*20).

Now keep ahead on the D788 through the resort of **Ploumanac'h**★ (229km/142mi ✝✣🄰✕⊕🖝wc) and continue to **Trégastel-Plage**★ (230km/143mi 🄰△✕🖳⊕ 🖝wc) from where Walk 21 takes you along this wonderful coast. Remain on the D788 and follow signs for Trébeurden along the Breton Corniche, which runs beside the beautiful Pink Granite Coast, illustrated on pages 19 and 126-127 (🖝🝙*P*21). From **Trébeurden**★ (242km/150mi 🄰△✕🖳⊕🖝wc) follow 'Lannion', to leave on the D65 (🝙). Re-enter **Lannion** (251km/156mi) and follow 'Toutes Directions', by river. Turn right to cross the river at 253km/157mi, then bear left ('Autres Directions'). Finally, head right on the D11 for Ploubezre, to complete the circuit.

7 THE CHATEAUBRIAND ROAD

Rennes • Châteaugiron • Vitré • Fougères • Combourg • Dinan • Cap Fréhel • Lamballe • Jugon-les-Lacs • Broöns • Bécherel • Les Iffs • Rennes

420km/261mi; 11h driving (a two-day tour)

On route: Picnic (see pages 11-15) 22; Walk 19

The best way to break this circuit into two one-day tours is as follows:

Shorter tour 1: Follow the notes below as far as the Château de la Bourbansais at Pleugueneuc (page 43). Then, instead of turning right on the N137, go left. After 3km/2mi enter St-Domineuc and, 6km/4mi further on, turn right on the D20 in Tinténiac for Bécherel. Pass through La Baussaine after 5km/3mi. Turn left in Bécherel (3.5km/2mi beyond La Baussaine) and continue the tour to its end at Rennes (see page 45).

Shorter tour 2: Begin at any convenient point between Pleugueneuc and Bécherel and follow the tour as described, until you reach Bécherel (page 45). Instead of turning right on the D27 for Rennes, cross over and keep straight ahead on the D20 for Tinténiac, passing La Baussaine in 3.5km/2mi. Turn left on the N137 in Tinténiac (5km/3mi beyond La Baussaine). Pass St-Domineuc after 6km/4mi and carry on for another 3km/2mi to Pleugueneuc. Pass the Château de la Bourbansais on the right and continue the tour to Dinan, as described on page 43.

This tour largely follows the *route touristique* 'Chateaubriand', named after Brittany's foremost man of letters, François-René de Chateaubriand. It takes you through the *départements* of Ille-et-Vilaine and Côtes-d'Armor in eastern Brittany, visiting most of its châteaux and important monuments. The majority can be visited during part of the year (at a price): details may be obtained at the Tourist Office in Rennes. The drive begins in **Rennes★** (♣❖▲✕ ▒⊕Mwc) or, rather, on the N136 expressway which encircles it.

Leave the expressway to the southeast, taking the D463 to **Châteaugiron** (11km/7mi ♣▪❖▲✕▒⊕), where you turn right by the church for Janzé (D92). Turn left in **Janzé** (23km/14mi) on the D41 ('Autres Directions'), then bear left again for Le Theil, still on the D41. At 24km/15mi keep ahead at crossroads, signposted 'La Roche aux Fées'. Pass through **Le Theil** and, after 3km/2mi, turn left by the furniture showrooms (34km/21mi) on the D341, again following 'La Roche aux Fées'. Keep ahead at crossroads; after 3km/2mi you reach **La Roche aux Fées** ('the Fairies' Rock')★, one of the finest megalithic monuments in Brittany (▐▌⊼; see drawing on the title page).

Carry on northwards to **Essé** and, at 40km/25mi, turn right, then left, on the D99 for Piré-sur-Seiche. In the hamlet of **Boistrudan** (43km/27mi), turn left on the D32 for Piré. Follow the road to the left through **Piré**, then turn right at the crossroads (48km/30mi), to leave on the D777.

After 3km/2mi keep ahead at the crossroads for Vitré (and Paris!). Some 8km/5mi further on, pass through **Louvigné** (♨). Drive beneath the expressway and come into **Vitré★** (69km/43mi ♨⛪✣▲✕➧⊕🎦MWC), famed for its superb mediaeval castle and exceptionally well-preserved Old Town. Follow 'Centre Ville' and turn left to pass by the castle. Cross the river Vilaine and turn right along the Rue de Fougères, to leave on the D178 following 'Fougères'.

The castle at **Fougères★** (100km/62mi ♨⛪✣▲△✕➧⊕🎦MWC), one of the most massive still standing in Europe, has had a stormy history. In spite of all its fortifications, it has often been taken. To reach it, follow 'Centre Ville' and 'Château', then turn left along the Boulevard de Rennes. Leave Fougères to the north, initially following 'Avranches', then 'St-Malo' (D155).

Pass through the region known as Coglès (🌲 at 111km/69mi), in the direction of Antrain. But at 126km/78mi turn left on the D796 for Tremblay and Combourg. Keep ahead after 1.6km/1mi at the crossroads in **Tremblay**, following 'Bazouges-La-P.' and 'Combourg'. In **Bazouges** (134km/83mi) follow signs for Combourg, but beware of *priorité à droite* at the first junction. At the next junction turn right, to continue heading west, still on the D796.

Combourg★ (151km/94mi ⛪▲✣✕➧⊕) is a long narrow town. Follow 'Rennes' as far as the haunted castle, where François-René de Chateaubriand spent the two lonely and gloomy teenage years which he described in his *Mémoires d'Outre-Tombe* ('Memories from Beyond the Grave'). Turn right now for Dinan on the D794, still heading west. After passing through **Meillac**, turn left at 158km/98mi for Pleugueneuc (D75). After 5km/3mi you will see on your right the Château de la Bourbansais (⛪).

At the T-junction in **Pleugueneuc** turn right on the N137. At 167km/104mi join the D794 and follow 'Dinan' (🌲 3km/2mi along). After 10km/6mi, in **Lanvallay**, take the right-hand lane at traffic lights, to go straight ahead, then turn left at the junction with the N176. Bear left at a fork, cross the viaduct, and enter **Dinan★** (179km/111mi ♨⛪✣▲△✕➧⊕🎦MWC*P22*). Like Vitré, Dinan has preserved its ramparts, within which a wealth of beautifully-restored ancient buildings creates a tourist paradise. Walk 19 begins and ends here (photographs pages 21 and 117).

Leave Dinan on the N176, following signs for St-Brieuc. At 184km/114mi turn right at the roundabout, onto the D794 (again signposted 'St-Brieuc'), then continue in the direction of Corseul. After 5km/3mi make a short diversion

(0.8km/0.5mi) to the left, signposted '**Temple de Mars**'. It is not a temple, but a tower, and one of the very few Roman remains (**☖**) still standing in Brittany. Return to the D794 and turn left. In **Plancoët** (198km/123mi), be careful. Ignore the first turning on the right (D768 to St-Malo); take the *next* turning on the right, the D19, for St-Cast-le-Guildo. At the next junction turn right again and, thereafter, follow signs for St-Cast and St-Lormel. Turn left at 206km/128mi onto the D786 for St-Brieuc. After 1.6km/1mi keep straight ahead for Erquy and Matignon. Bear left in **Matignon** for Erquy and Cap Fréhel, still on the D786, then bear right. After 3km/2mi you reach the sea.

At 217km/135mi turn right on the D16 for Cap Fréhel, and, 3km/2mi further on, follow 'Fort La Latte'. Pass through **Plévenon** and continue to follow 'Fort La Latte'. At 227km/141mi pass a picnic site (**☶**) and turn right, after 3km/2mi parking in the car park. From here follow a footpath for a view of **Fort La Latte** (**☖☎**; see drawing on page 2). The menhir you pass has been given the name of 'Gargantua's Finger'. Drive back to the D16 and then turn right for **Cap Fréhel★** (**☎☶**). After 1.6km/1mi you must pay to continue out along the cape; the main tour turns left on the D34a (signposted 'St-Brieuc'). Follow the coastal road for 9km/6mi, through beautiful scenery. Beyond **Sables d'Or** take the D34 to the left and, at 243km/151mi, turn right on the D786. After 1.6km/1mi bear left on the D34 for St-Brieuc. Pass the junction with the D768 in **La Couture** (248km/154mi) and, 1.6km/1mi further on, a picnic site (**☶**). At 251km/156mi look out for the **Château de Bien-Assis** (**☖**) on the left, beyond which you turn left on the D17a (**☶**) for St-Alban and Lamballe. Bypass St-Alban and, at 259km/161mi, take the last exit at the roundabout, for Lamballe (D791).

Nearing **Lamballe★** (269km/167mi **☩▲▲✕☕⊕M**wc), take the second turning out of the roundabout. Turn left at the first traffic lights, and right at the second (for Moncontour). Follow signs 'Moncontour' and 'Loudéac' 1.6km/1mi further on (D768). Do not go into Moncontour: turn left at 285km/177mi on the D6 to Collinée and Trédaniel. Keep ahead at the crossroads, but take the next road on the left, at 287km/178mi. This is the D25 to Trébry. You pass the 16th-century **Château de la Touche-Trébry** (**☖**) on your left after 3km/2mi. Continue on the D25 through **Trébry** and **St-Glen** (ignoring the road on the right to Collinée). Turn left in St-Glen for Plenée-Jugon and Lamballe (295km/183mi), and bear right at the next junction. At 296km/184mi cross over the D14 and, still on the D25, continue towards Plenée-Jugon.

After 5km/3mi turn right (Plenée-Jugon is signposted, if you can spot the sign!). At 304km/189mi turn left at the junction with the D792 and enter **Plenée-Jugon**. Pass the church and follow signs for Jugon (D792). After 5km/3mi cross over the expressway and follow the D792 into **Jugon-les-Lacs** (314km/195mi ⛺🏔△✕📻). Two dams across the river Arguenon provide Jugon with long lakes to the north and south. Leave the picturesque town by following 'Lac'. Fork sharp right (D16) on reaching the southern lake, for Dolo and Broöns. At 317km/197mi turn left in front of **Dolo** church, following 'Broöns'. Turn left towards Rennes at the crossroads and, at 322km/200mi, cross over the railway line and drive beside the expressway. After 1.6km/1mi bear right for Broöns; bear right again 3km/2mi further on to enter **Broöns** (327km/203mi ❖).

Leave Broöns in the direction of Rennes. Briefly join the N12 expressway, but leave it after 1.6km/1mi, taking the D25 for Caulnes. In **Caulnes** cross the railway and turn right on the D766. Turn left by the church and follow the D25 (signposted 'Guitté' and 'Plouasne'), soon passing the **Château de Couëllan** (🏛). At 345km/214mi turn right in **Guitté** and take the D89 into **Médréac**. Go by the church, passing to the right of the village and under the railway on the D61, heading for **St-M'Hervon**. Some 1.6km/1mi beyond St-M'Hervon pass the 12th-century **Château de Montauban** (🏛) on the right. Soon turn left on the expressway and, almost at once, leave it at the next junction (D71 to Bécherel). At 362km/225mi pass through **Landujan** (⛪) and, at 369km/229mi, bear right at the junction by the telecommunications tower for Bécherel, soon passing the **Château de Caradeuc** (🏛) on your left.

Go through **Bécherel** (370km/230mi) and, at the crossroads, turn right on the D27 for Rennes. After 6km/4mi turn left on the D221 for Les Iffs. Pass to the right of the church in **Les Iffs**, to reach the **Château de Montmuran** (🏛). Here Brittany's greatest warrior, Bertrand Duguesclin, was dubbed knight in 1354 and married in 1372. From here return to the D27 (380km/236mi). Turn left for Rennes, noting a fine manor house after 1.6km/1mi in **La Chapelle Chaussée**.

At 402km/250mi follow 'Rennes' at the roundabout and join the N136. Follow 'Autres Directions' (or 'Centre Ville', if you intend to visit Rennes). At 420km/261mi you reach the Châteaugiron exit, where the tour began.

✿ Walking

Walking in Brittany is neither strenuous nor demanding. Indeed the 'serious hiker' may find Brittany tame. But the rambler looking for something less adventurous than the Alps or Pyrenees will find Brittany a paradise. There are thousands of miles of waymarked walks, including more miles of the Grande Randonnée long distance footpaths than in any other region of France. With so much to choose from, it has been possible to select a score of really splendid walks of great beauty and variety, taking you to some of the most interesting sights in Brittany. There are walks to suit every taste, from very short strolls (see the picnic section on pages 11-15) to day-long hikes. These longer walks usually have one or more shorter alternatives — good half-day rambles.

To choose a walk that appeals to you, you might begin by looking at the touring map. Here you can see at a glance the overall terrain, the roads, and the location of the walks. Flipping through the book, you will see that there is at least one photograph for every walk. Having selected one or two potential excursions from the map and the photographs, turn to the relevant walk. At the top of the page you will find planning information: distance/time, grade, equipment, and how to get there/return.

When you are on your walk, you will find that the text begins with an introduction and then quickly turns to a detailed description of the route. Times are given for reaching certain points in the walk. Note that I walk quite quickly on the flat: compare your pace with mine on one of the short walks before setting off on a long hike. Remember that times do not take into account any time not spent walking (other than for getting your breath back on hills!) If using public transport, allow plenty of time for catching your return bus or train.

N uisances
Dogs pose the only problem. Not that I have been bitten by one, but I have been frightened. They are there to see off strangers, and that's what they do. I have invested in an ultrasonic dog deterrent. You may like to do the same: for details and price list write to: Dazer Freepost, London SW11 6BR.

W hat to take

For many walks, walking boots are best. The tracks you will be following are often roughly-surfaced and uneven, sometimes with loose stones lying on them. No matter how careful you are, there is always the possibility of twisting your ankle. With boots you have some protection against this, and the chance of getting back to your car. You will also at some stage have the problem of mud to cope with. If you cannot face boots, then trainers may be preferable to shoes, since the same stones and mud will damage your good shoes terribly, but take a bandage in case you do put your ankle out. Unless the text specifies 'any comfortable footwear', *never* walk in sandals.

In summer you will need a long-sleeved shirt for protection against the sun, and for the same reason a sunhat and sun cream. I prefer long trousers. It is tempting to wear shorts in the summer, but not only do you run the risk of sunburn on the backs of your legs, on the wilder walks you will get nettled and scratched. Oddly enough, shorts win in warm rain. Not hanging below your anorak they do not get wet, and legs are easier to dry than trousers. If the walk includes a beach, take a towel and swimwear, but make sure that the beach is safe if you intend to bathe. Many of the exposed beaches of Finistère are extremely dangerous, and bathing is forbidden. Sound waterproof clothing is essential. You will need a small rucksack, first-aid kit, plastic cups, up-to-date bus timetables, water and food. A compass, whistle and torch are always advisable. Bird lovers should try to have lightweight binoculars. One of my eccentricities is to take a small pair of garden secateurs — invaluable for cutting away encroaching branchlets which obstruct narrow paths. **For each walk in the book, the *minimum* equipment is listed.**

M aps

The walking routes described have been overprinted in green on IGN 1:25,000 maps from the 'Série Bleue'. We have reduced them to a scale of 1:40,000. While roads, tracks, railway lines, etc are easily identified, you might wish to review the following symbols:

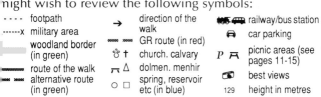

`- - - -` footpath	→ direction of the walk	railway/bus station
`------x` military area		car parking
woodland border (in green)	GR route (in red)	
	⚲ † church. calvary	P ⊓ picnic areas (see pages 11-15)
route of the walk	⊓ △ dolmen. menhir	
alternative route (in green)	○ □ spring, reservoir etc (in blue)	best views
		129 height in metres

1 PARISH CLOSES OF ST-THEGONNEC AND GUIMILIAU

Distance: 19.2km/12mi; 4h50min   **Grade:** moderate

Equipment: comfortable shoes of any kind, sunhat, suncream, raingear, picnic, water

How to get there and return: 🚂 to St-Thégonnec from Morlaix or Brest. 🚗 to St-Thégonnec railway station, which can be reached by leaving the N12 expressway at the St-Thégonnec exit, and driving south on the D118, by-passing the village itself. Park in front of the station.

Shorter walks

1 St-Thégonnec — Luzec Calvary — St-Thégonnec (13.8km/8.6mi; 3h15min; easy; equipment and access as main walk). Follow the main walk as far as the Luzec Calvary, reached in 2h23min. Ignore the right turn, and continue along the road southwards for nearly 2km/1.2mi, passing a road on the right, and keeping left at the following junction (by a cross). Pass one more road on the left. On reaching the crossroads by yet another calvary, keep straight ahead and in 100m/yds turn left for the station.

2 Guimiliau — St-Aubin — Roc'h Toull — Guimiliau (9.3km/5.8mi; 2h30min; grade and equipment as main walk). 🚂 (from Morlaix or Brest) or 🚗 (N12 expressway and then D31) to Guimiliau. Start out at the church square (the 3h35min-point in the main walk), and follow the directions for the main walk as far as the road junction reached 12 minutes beyond the hamlet of St-Aubin. Turn left and follow the road northwards for 1.7km/1mi. You will pass two roads on the left, the second by a cross, and then a road on the right to Rohellou (as well as the occasional track), before coming to a track on the left 20m/yds before the Luzec Calvary. Turn left on this track and follow the main walk (from the 2h23min-point) back to Guimiliau.

In 1581 two centuries of rivalry began between the neighbouring Léon villages of St-Thégonnec and Guimiliau, as each strove to outdo the other in the ornamentation of its parish church and churchyard. Now they are two of the finest parish closes in the whole of Brittany. On this walk you visit them both, and cross the verdant valley of the river Penzé that separates them.

To begin the walk, turn left on leaving the station and pass in front of the Celtavel factory. In **10min** turn right at a T-junction, signposted 'Pont ar Roz' and 'Guimiliau'. In 150m/yds you will come to crossroads and a calvary. Go straight over and, in four minutes, pass a track on the left (along which you will eventually return). In a further minute turn right along a gravel track (**15min**). Seven minutes later, turn right again at a T-junction, along a similar track, and pass the hamlet of Bodéniry (or 'Bodiniéry'). Soon you will arrive at another T-junction. Once more turn right and, in three minutes, turn left at the next junction, to pass an elaborate calvary after 200m/yds.

Take the first road on the left in about nine minutes and walk to the left of a little brook, away from the large silo nd towards Calafres. In two minutes, when the road bends left to the farm, bear right along a gravel track and cross the brook. In four minutes keep straight ahead, ignoring a track on the right. Ahead is the water tower of St-Thégonnec. Brittany is full of water towers, and they are useful for orientation. In eight minutes you come to a crossroads. Keep on the track straight ahead and, in three minutes, follow the track as it bends to the left and then to the right, a minute later ignoring a track on the left.

In seven minutes you will reach another calvary, at a road junction (**1h02min**). Ignore the road to the left, and keep straight ahead. On your right you can see the belfry of St-Thégonnec's church. In ten minutes turn right at a T-junction and walk into the village, finally climbing up the Rue de Chapellendy to reach the church (**1h23min**). Its impact is breathtaking, whether it be the calvary (1610), or the ossuary (built in 1676 and perhaps the best Renaissance building in Brittany), with Jacques Lespaignol's almost life-size carving of the body of Christ being laid in the Holy Sepulchre. Within the church this is outdone by erel's pulpit of 1683, one of the finest carvings in the province.

Pass to the left of the church, then turn right in front of the Bar es Sports. Take the first street

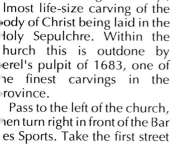

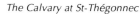
The Calvary at St-Thégonnec

on the left, facing another calvary, between the *quincaillerie* (ironmongers) and the Logis de France. Cross over the main road at the end, and continue down a country lane opposite. The lane bends to the left, then in 50m/yds turns sharply to the right. At this point leave the metalled road and continue ahead along a rough track for nine minutes — as far as the junction with a narrow road. Cross this road, turn left, and walk parallel to it along a narrow path which diverges from the road to reach an old mill (**1h39min**).

Since leaving the village we have been following the GR380. You may have noticed the white and red waymarks, and they will help you identify your route. Now they lead you past a tarmac road on the left and beside the mill-race, up a grassy path to the D712. Turn left and walk up the main road for 50m/yds, then cross over and turn right up a road signposted 'Menhars/Coslen/Bouges'. At Menhars the road bends left and heads for a calvary which you may recognise. Turn right at the calvary and retrace your steps as far as the next calvary (**1h56min**), where you now turn right and descend to Coslen. In three minutes follow the road round to the left, to Bouges, where it will wind right and left. Take no notice of the turning to the right, and continue to follow the GR signs.

After Bouges the tarmac ends, and you are on a gravel track (**2h04min**). The track twists right, left, and right again for two minutes. Care is needed now, for here you leave the main track and turn right along a path that descends through woodland. It is well waymarked: in addition to the GR marks, there is also a yellow arrow. (If still you fail to notice the turning, a white and red cross by a pile of wood tells you that you are going the wrong way.) In another two minutes cross a little brook and climb up to the junction with a tarmac road (**2h12min**). Turn left, and walk uphill past a farm. In 11 minutes (**2h23min**) you come to another fine calvary, that of Luzec. Follow the road as it bends left behind it.

Shorter walk 1 continues straight ahead here. The main walk turns right down a gravel track after 20m/yds (ignoring the GR cross). The rock outcrop ahead is known as Roc'h Toull. In 13 minutes you come to an old mill

2h36min). Turn right and follow the track between buildings (taking heed of the 'Danger' signs), then double back to cross the stream, after which you will see GR signs once more. The track bends to the right, as you ignore a path on the left. Down here by the stream is probably the best place to picnic although, if it should it be raining, there is a dry cave in the side of Roc'h Toull — some 50m/yds further on, to the left. You may wish to explore this cave (signposted 'Grotte') in any case. Afterwards, return to the junction and turn left, to continue along the original track. In nine minutes bear right at a junction of tracks, towards a farm, beyond which the track is metalled. Ignore a track on the left, and follow the tarmac to the next junction (in front of trees), where you turn right. Some 0m/yds further on, bear left at the next junction (**3h**).

In 14 minutes there is a well bearing a crucifix on your left, and a road on the right. Ignore that road. Formerly the GR went along there, but the way is now blocked. Keep straight ahead, passing roads on the left to Keranhéroff and Keranfors. Follow the road round to the right, to its junction with the D31 (by a cross; **3h23min**). Turn left; then take the second turning on the right ('Restvez'), and turn left when you come to a T-junction.

In two minutes you arrive at Guimiliau's church (**3h35min**), which boasts the most splendid calvary in all Brittany, completed in 1581 and sporting no less than 200 figures. Also remarkable is the south porch built of Kersanton granite in 1606. Within the church the carved font cover and another Lerel pulpit claim attention.

Pass the church and turn right into the square. Then turn left in front of the Loveburger Bar, to follow the Rue des Bruyères to its junction with the D31. Cross over and continue down the country road opposite for 300m/yds, to a crossroads. Turn right here, in the direction of 'Gare de St-Thégonnec' (**3h49min**). In a further 300m/yds ignore a road on the right which crosses the railway line, and carry on downhill, to re-cross the river Penzé. Follow the road round to the left, and turn right when you come to a T-junction, walking away from Pont ar Roz. In 250m/yds turn left at the crossroads and pass the hamlet of St-Aubin. Take the next turning on the right, a narrow road which quickly turns to track. In 12 minutes turn right at a road junction. (*Shorter walk 2 turns left at this junction.*) Pass the calvary that you saw soon after the start of the walk, cross the road to St-Thégonnec and, after 100m/yds, turn left for 'Gare', to return to the station (**4h50min**).

2 POINTE DE PEN-HIR

See photograph page 23

Distance: 20.3km/12.6mi; 4h46min   **Grade:** moderate

Equipment: walking boots if wet, otherwise comfortable shoes or trainers, sunhat, suncream, raingear, picnic, water, swimwear (but check that bathing is permitted), towel

How to get there and return: 🚌 to Camaret from Quimper or Brest, both of which can be reached by train. The bus stop is outside the Café de la Paix, by the harbour. 🚗: Camaret is on the west coast of Finistère at the end of the Crozon Peninsula. Park in the centre of the town, beside the harbour.

Shorter walk: Camaret — Pointe de Pen-Hir — Camaret (12.3km/7.6mi; 3h15min; grade, equipment, access as main walk). Follow the main walk as far as the car park at the end of Veryarc'h Beach (the 2h35min point). Turn left here and follow the road to the hamlet of Kermeur which you reach in ten minutes. Keep straight ahead as far as the T-junction where you turn right. In another minute fork right along the Rue de Kermeur. On reaching the roundabout, cross over and turn right along the Rue Pasteur, towards the church. Turn left at the church and go downhill to the harbour.

Camaret's claim to fame seems to be that an American engineer named Fulton demonstrated the first submarine here in 1801. Our interest lies in its wonderful wild coast, littered with every manner of abandoned fortification, climaxing — if you can tear yourself away from Pen-Hat Beach — in the dramatic Tas de Pois islets of the Pointe de Pen-Hir. Also en route in both the main and the Shorter walk are the alignments of menhirs at Lagatjar.

To begin the walk, face the sea: turn left and walk beside the harbour. At the end of the harbour turn right and walk along the mole, to visit the Rocamadour chapel (built in the 17th century for pilgrims landing at Camaret on their way to the great shrine at Rocamadour) and the curious fortress designed by Vauban (also 17th century; photograph page 23), which houses a naval museum. Retrace your steps along the mole, then keep straight ahead to walk up the hill behind the beach (**25min**). Cross diagonally a grassy, furnished picnic area (**P**4), and turn right on leaving. In one minute fork left and follow the path up the hill — not the steps down to the beach. Cross a concrete footbridge in front of a house and, in another minute, keep straight ahead, ignoring the track to the left.

After two minutes fork right on the narrow path going slightly downhill. Three minutes later you come to the first of many ruins of fortifications you will pass on this walk. Follow the path up steps on your left, round a house (beneath the bridge leading to the entrance), and go on up more steps. Then bear left and continue along the cliffs

In **41min** (some five minutes after leaving the last fort) the path goes by more ruins. *Care is needed here —especially if you have children, or are deep in absorbing conversation, or if conditions are other than perfect.* This next short stretch is exceptionally dangerous, because the path goes straight across ground littered with large holes which drop into the blockhouses. To your right lies the Brest roadstead. This region is the home of the French navy. At the extreme left, across the roadstead, you can see St Matthew's Point (Pointe de St-Mathieu).

In three minutes the path swings left, to head south. On your right is the Pointe du Toulinguet, with its lighthouse and another fort. Your path follows the curls of the cliff-edge for five minutes. Then, becoming more a grassy track, it begins to head inland between tall gorse bushes. On joining a tarmac road, turn right and, at the next junction, turn right again (opposite the entrance to the Auberge de Jeunesse). Very soon the road bends left and, in two minutes, passes a wide gravel track on your left. Some 20m/yds beyond this track, fork right and follow a footpath diagonally across a field, at the back of a pebble bay.

Having crossed the field, the path rejoins the road at a junction, **1h** into the walk. Cross the road and go down the road opposite for 50m/yds; then, before you come to a row of posts and a notice board, bear right along a footpath. It leads you to a glorious beach — the Anse de Pen-Hat (**P**5). Either go down steps and walk along the beach, or walk along the low cliff above the beach, which avoids an awkward scramble back up. Should you wish to go for a swim, be warned that bathing here is dangerous, as it is so often along this coast.

Turn left when you reach the large boulders at the far end of the beach, and climb away from the sea. Follow an uphill path running at right angles to the coast, to a strange ruined building with several round towers — the Manoir de Coëcilian, for many years the home of the poet Saint-Pol-Roux, who was shot here in 1940 by a drunken German sergeant-major. Pass to its left, then follow a track to and through a car park. On reaching a tarmac road, turn right. In 50m/yds turn left along a short track, which brings you to the most important collection of menhirs in Finistère, the Alignements de Lagatjar (**1h22min**).

Retrace your steps to the towered ruin and turn left. Walk along a footpath at the right of a line of houses, then keep forward past the Museum of the Battle of the Atlantic, again beside the cliffs. At **2h** you will be near the Pointe

de Pen-Hir. The first object of interest is the monument
to the Breton fighters for Free France during World War
II. Bear left beyond the monument, to continue round the
cliffs. You come to the end of a tarmac road, where there
is a viewing platform with chart and telescopes, overlooking the off-shore rocks known as the Tas de Pois ('Heaps
of Peas') … another fine spot for a picnic on a quiet day.

Now follow the path on the far side of the promontory
northwards. In five minutes bear right, to walk round the
next bay, Veryarc'h Beach. In six minutes you join a
tarmac road and pass in front of the Bar du Veryarc'h.
Two minutes later leave the tarmac again: walk up a path
behind the beach. In five minutes pass a little quarry on
your left and bear right to continue beside the sea. Five
minutes later you have to get round a small gorge, so
follow the path inland, to a road and car park (**2h35min**).
(*If you are doing the Shorter walk, turn left here.*)

Continue on a wide track round the end of the gorge
and back to the cliffs. The track goes round another bay
and promontory, the Pointe de la Tavelle, and on past a

small island (**3h**). In three minutes pass an overgrown track on the left and go between wooden posts designed (not very successfully) to deter cars. One minute later you meet more of the same, and a wall and track on the left. Keep straight ahead and, in three minutes, go by the Pointe de Portzen to the right. In three minutes pass a walled field on your left and, as you round the next little bay, you can see over on your right a huge bay — the Anse de Dinan, with the vast sandy beach of Kerziguénou.

Six minutes beyond the walled field, the track forks (**3h17min**), at a point half way round the little shingle bay. Bear left here. The track you are leaving continues past a promontory and down to that vast beach, but your way is towards a line of pine trees and a white rock outcrop behind them. In three minutes turn left at a T-junction, and walk between wooden posts, with the outcrop now on your right and the pines on your left. In another three minutes the track bears left (where an overgrown, barely-distinguishable track goes off to the right) and shortly bends right to take you northwards, past a track on the left and into the hamlet of Kerguélen. At the junction with a tarmac road, turn left and, in four minutes, turn right at the next junction, in the neighbouring hamlet of Lannilien. Walk downhill, passing the chapel of St-Julien (up a short road on the left). Beyond the chapel, climb to the junction with the D8, passing two tracks to the right en route.

At the junction (**3h38min**) turn left. The D8 is a busy road; although it's not usually advisable, you are probably better walking on the right-hand side, where the verge is wider. In four minutes you pass a sign warning of a school; 20m/yds beyond the sign, turn right along a track (un-metalled at time of writing). In five minutes go over a crossroads (ignoring a narrow track to the right) and up the road opposite. Stay on this road for four minutes, then turn right along the D55. After 50m/yds turn left along a narrow road signposted 'Rigounou' and bear right at the next T-junction, in front of a farm. Stay on this road as it bends to the left and right and then, four minutes later, to the left again. You approach Lambézen. As you enter the village (**4h04min**) there are streets to the right and left, but keep straight ahead. Do the same at the next crossroads and, three minutes later, you will come to the junction with the D355.

Turn right now and, almost at once, bear left. Within 10m/yds turn left again, up a tarred track. When the tarring stops, the track forks into two paths (**4h12min**). (The next bit is slightly tricky. If you have any difficulty, please read the next paragraph, 'At 4h26min …'.) Both paths take you to the same place, but take the one to the right; it is the more interesting. You come to steps on the left: climb them, then circle a house. Behind the house, clamber up a barely-distinguishable footpath for a metre or two — to the top of the bank, where you will join a well-trodden path. Turn right, and follow the path through grassy country round the Pointe Ste-Barbe and along the cliffs.

At **4h26min** the path runs beside the D355. (If you have not been able to find your way behind the house for any reason, return to the D355 and turn right — ie, towards Camaret. By following the D355 for about eight minutes or 0.6km/0.4mi, you can gain access to the path at this point.) In one minute descend sharply for a short distance to cross a small valley at the back of a shingle beach. Make your way through quite thick, tall bushes for a couple of minutes, before climbing out of the valley (**4h30min**). In nine minutes you are above the port of Camaret, and the path forks. Go right, descending between houses. In 50m/yds pass a road on the left, as the path widens — first to a gravel track and then to a metalled road. A minute later turn right at the junction, to reach the car park/bus stop five minutes later (**4h46min**).

Walk 3 and Picnic 6:
Sea pinks contrast
with a turquoise
ocean at the
Plage de la Palue.

3 MORGAT — PEARL OF THE CROZON

See also photograph page 22

Distance: 16.5km/10.3mi; 3h53min   **Grade:** easy

Equipment: walking boots if wet, otherwise comfortable shoes or trainers, sunhat, suncream, raingear, picnic, water, swimwear (but check whether bathing is permitted), towel

How to get there and return: 🚌 to Crozon, then on foot to Morgat, the chic beach resort adjacent to Crozon. Buses from both Brest and Quimper stop at Crozon. Unfortunately the bus stop is about 3km from the start of the walk. 🚗 to Crozon in western Finistère; then turn left for the beach resort of Morgat. There is a limited amount of car parking space in Morgat, which may be at a premium during July and August.

The walk begins and ends at the most chic beach resort in western Finistère. It goes at first through an extensive wooded region, visits a tiny inscribed dolmen, then continues along an unbelievably unspoiled coast of long sand beaches, finally returning across quiet countryside.

Start by walking down to the sea front at Morgat. Turn right and make your way to the end of the beach; then follow the road round towards the harbour. Before reaching it you will notice the post office on your right and, beside it, a narrow road going up the hill. Turn right to ascend this road. (All references to time during the following instructions start from this point.)

Follow the road sharply round to the left after 20m/yds. Pass two roads on the right and a gravel track on the left, before joining a gravel track ahead, signposted 'Allée du Phare'. Soon you are at a crossroads. The Allée du Phare

goes on ahead to the lighthouse, but here you must turn right along the 'Allée du Ménez Kador'. This is a very wide track, lined with houses, and may well be asphalted one day. Pass a number of *allées* until, not far beyond the 'Impasse de Ménez Kador' on the left, the track acquires a bitumen surface. Keep straight ahead and, two minutes after crossing over the Allée du Bois de Quenvel, turn left at a T-junction in front of houses, along a somewhat overgrown track between gorse bushes. In a further two minutes fork left, avoiding a gate on the right. In three minutes you come to a wider, crossing track, where you turn right. In four minutes this track bends to the right and, a minute later, you turn left at a junction, following a fine gravel road and heading almost due south.

In ten minutes (**37min** after starting the walk) pass a track on the left, then one on the right. Three minutes later go over a smaller crossing track and, in two and four minutes, ignore tracks to the left. Pass between houses and gardens, and go over another crossing track. In five minutes cross yet another track. The further along you go, the more the surface of your track deteriorates, eventually becoming quite grassy, as you continue to ignore one more track to right and two to the left.

After **1h** walking, the bushes give place to small trees, and your path is more overgrown. To your right you can see the islands off the Pointe de Pen-Hir (Walk 2) known as the Tas de Pois ('Heaps of Peas'). And now you come to a T-junction of paths in front of some trees. Turn right and, in a couple of minutes, you reach the farming hamlet of St-Norgard. Follow the path, which broadens now, round the buildings. On coming to a junction, turn right along a gravel track, passing a house on your left. In some 200m/yds you reach another junction, in front of a little stone shed. Turn right here, along a better, wider track, and follow it towards the converted windmill dwelling shown on page 22. In four minutes (**1h13min**) turn left along the D255. Three minutes later, ignore a track on the left and the road to Ménez-Guen on the right. Pass two more tracks to the left and then look out for two posts on your left (**1h20min**). Follow the path between them for 50m/yds, to a tiny dolmen. The upright stone on the left bears mysterious engravings — some Roman numerals and a strange drawing underneath.

Return to the road and turn left. In 150m/yds turn right, along a road signposted 'Keravel'. After another 150m/yds, turn left down a tarmac road. Follow it round past another windmill and, in five minutes, turn left at a T-junction. After 20m/yds turn right in Kergonan, to reach a T-junction with a gravel track a minute later. Turn right and follow this track as it bends to the left and heads towards the sea. In six minutes turn right at another T-junction with an even wider track. Pass a path off to the left almost at once, followed by a drive with a chain across it. Turn left down the next track, which takes you to the top of the cliff. Ahead you can see the islet of Guénéron and, beyond it, the famous 'Heaps of Peas'.

Turn right and follow the path running diagonally towards the edge of the cliffs. You round a stony bay. Cross the headland and join a crossing track, where you turn left (**2h**). In 50m/yds leave the track (which now goes back inland) and fork left down a footpath, to proceed (with care) beside the edge of the cliff. Below you is the beautiful long, wide beach shown on pages 56-57, the

Plage de la Palue. Either go down to the beach and walk along it to the far end, or follow this path above it for some 2.3km/1.4mi. Twice the path descends to cross tiny brooks and climbs past a car park. Take no notice of the track to the right leading to la Palue. Now your path also becomes a gravel track. Stay parallel to the sea and ignore a second track heading inland, beyond a little house.

After half an hour (**2h35min**) cut across the headland of Pointe de Kerdra and continue behind (or across) a second bay. If you elect to stay on the cliff, follow the *sentier côtier* (coastal path) as it circles an area of fenced-off dunes and continues to the left of woodland. Should you have made your way down to the beach, be warned: bathing is forbidden here on account of the strong currents.

Keep straight ahead beyond the end of the beach (**2h51min**), until you are level with the Pointe de Lost Marc'h. Here you will see a path running inland from the ruins of a building on the headland. Turn right here, and head for the hamlet of Lost Marc'h, passing to the right of stones and a menhir on the way (**3h**).

Pass a barrier and a notice forbidding bathing, and enter Lost Marc'h. Keep straight ahead through the hamlet and, in nine minutes, pass a road on the right, as well as several gravel tracks. Take care on this road; it is quite busy with people driving to and from the beach. In 11 minutes ignore a road on the left and, two minutes later, a track on the right. After another three minutes (**3h25min**), bear left at a T-junction (on a bend). In three minutes ignore a road to the right and, 20m/yds further on, one to the left: bear right on a busy narrow road. In seven minutes turn right down the first tarmac road, after 70m/yds keeping right at a fork. Turn left after a further 100m/yds, along a gravel track. In 11 minutes you reach the junction with the D255, where you turn left. After 50m/yds turn right, go over one crossing road, and arrive back at the beach in Morgat, near your starting point (**3h53min**).

The 'chaos' at Huelgoat (Walk 4 and Picnic 7)

See photograph opposite

Distance: 13.8km/8.6mi; 3h36min   **Grade:** moderate

Equipment: walking boots if wet, otherwise comfortable shoes or trainers, sunhat, suncream, raingear, picnic, water

How to get there and return: 🚌 to Huelgoat. There is a daily, albeit infrequent, service between Morlaix and Carhaix which calls at Huelgoat. 🚗: Huelgoat, in eastern Finistère, lies just to the north of the D764. If your journey brings you via Morlaix, take the D769 south along the Queffleuth Valley. There is a large car park on the southeast shore of the lake at Huelgoat. This is taken as the starting point of the walk.

Short Walk: Huelgoat — Kerampeulven — Huelgoat (7.1km/4.4mi; 2h; grade, equipment, access as above). Follow the main walk as far as the menhir of Kerampeulven (about 1h25min) but, instead of turning right at the T-junction, follow the Grande Randonnée to the left. Halfway up the hill, the tarmac peters out, and you are on a wide gravel track. At the top of the hill the track narrows and forks. Leave the GR here, bearing left along a narrower gravel track. In two minutes ignore the narrow fork on the left; head downhill between bushes, with open views to the right. In another four minutes you reach a tarmac road (1h36min), where you turn left. Three minutes later, fork right and climb past houses. Beyond the houses the road reverts to a narrow track and begins its descent (1h43min; ignore a track on the right). Further down, the track is tarred and named 'Allée des Lauriers'. At the T-junction, turn left and follow the road past the *gendarmerie*. At the next junction, turn right along the D14 (1h51min). In four minutes you will reach the end of the lake, where you turn right and follow the shore back to the car park.

Some say it is the most beautiful inland place in Brittany, this village of Huelgoat beside a carp-filled lake and surrounded by beech woods and conifer plantations.

Begin the walk at the car park: follow the shore of the lake to its eastern end. Turn left again in front of the Café du Chaos. After 50m/yds, follow the sign 'La Roche Tremblante', going up the first street on the right (by a stone cross). As you climb, look over to your right at the 'chaos' of massive boulders choking the stream (see opposite). Almost at the top of the hill, leave the tarmac road and follow the signposted path to the right. Walk between the trees, towards the iron railings seen ahead, where steps will take you down to the huge 'Trembling Rock' (**20min**). Carry on down past the rock, to a prettily-sited picnic area (**P**7), and turn right along a footpath signposted 'Sentier des Amoureux' ('Lovers' Lane'), beside a little stream. Pass to the left of a timber-clad house; not far beyond it, turn left and cross over the stream, with a splendid view of the 'chaos'. Now the path forks. Take the Allée Violette, downhill to the right, and follow a beautiful wide path beside the stream. In a few minutes look out for steps ascending to the 'Stelle du Fusil' — a memorial to Resistance fighters shot here in 1944 (**30min**).

61

In five minutes you briefly leave the forest and turn left along the D769a. After 100m/yds, turn left and re-enter the forest along a path signposted 'Grotte d'Artus/Mare aux Sangliers/Camp d'Artus'. You have now joined the GR 380-37 and will have the benefit of the white and red waymarks for the next 50 minutes. Within 100m/yds ignore a path to the left signposted 'Camp d'Artus'; ignore also (for the time being) a similar path 50m/yds further on. Carry on for 200m/yds to La Mare aux Sangliers, the 'Wild Boars' Pool'. In a minute you will pass the Grotte d'Artus ('King Arthur's Cave') — not really a cave, but a place where huge boulders have tumbled and lodged against each other. In three minutes bear right along a tiny path (the signpost may be broken) down to the stream to look at the Mare aux Sangliers.

Retrace your steps now for four minutes, until you are back at the turning (now on your right), signposted 'Camp d'Artus'. The path (which is the other end of the Sentier des Amoureux) climbs gently through trees for several minutes. Follow the GR waymarks and the 'Camp d'Artus' sign, and bear right at a junction. At the top of the hill the forest has been cleared. Bear right along a track which sweeps round to the left. In eight minutes you reach the entrance to the Camp d'Artus (**1h05min**). Legend claims that this is the Breton 'Camelot', home to King Arthur and Queen Guinevere, and to the Knights of the Round Table. Sir Mortimer Wheeler's excavations here in 1938 showed it rather to be the site of a Gaulish village.

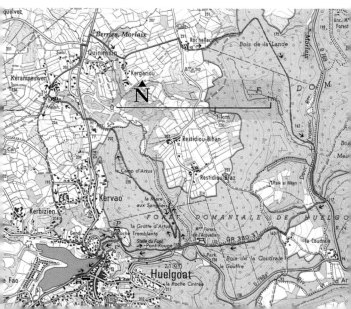

Cross the site and continue along a track, until you arrive at a signposted junction of tracks. Your way is now to the left, in the direction of Kerampeulven. After about 300m/yds you will leave the forest and cross over the D14 (**1h18min**). Follow the GR waymarks up the minor tarmac road opposite but, where the bitumen ends, leave the track: first bear left, and then right, along a woodland path beside gates decorated with a cockerel and a hen. After 200m/yds you arrive at the hamlet of Kerampeulven. Follow the road between the buildings until you pass the last house. Turn left immediately: in front of you stands a superb menhir. If you examine it closely, you will see that at some time in its history animals were engraved on it. Scholarly opinion seems to be that all drawings found on Breton megaliths post-date their original erection.

Continue along the road out of the hamlet and, in a few metres, come to a T-junction, where you turn right. *The Short walk bears left here*, as does the Grande Randonnée, so you will no longer have the assistance of its waymarks. Keep right in a few minutes, at a fork. At the next junction, ignore a road on your right. You have now almost regained the D14. Do not go on to the main road, however: bear slightly left at the junction, to walk parallel with the D14, along the old road. After 250m/yds turn right at a cross-roads. Walk 25m/yds to the D14 (**1h35min**) and turn left. Follow this main road for 100m/yds, then cross it and turn right, along a minor road with orange waymarks. In six minutes turn left at a T-junction; the route is no longer waymarked in orange, but in blue. After the initial bend, the road climbs for nine minutes to another T-junction. Turn right and, in 100m/yds, bear left, to pass the farm of Roc'hellec. The tarmac drive curls into the farmyard, but keep straight on, along a gravel track. After 50m/yds ignore a track on the left.

Three minutes after leaving the road (about 100m/yds after passing the farm), you come to a junction of tracks. Care is needed here. There appear at first to be two tracks, one bearing left (a continuation of the track you have been following) and one to the right (which leads into a meadow). In fact there are *three*. Straight ahead you can see a tree stump with a blue band and a faint blue arrow on it, and a beech tree with a sign forbidding shooting. Your way lies between the tree and the stump, and your path is overgrown compared with the other two, but with luck there will be tractor tracks to reassure you. After about 200m/yds, you will reach a good forest track, on a bend, where the blue route turns right. Your way, however, is to the left (**2h01min**).

You follow this forest track now for about half an hour. In some 500m/yds it turns southwest, and from then on it is downhill all the way. Occasionally (as by post no. 46) paths join your route, but ignore them. You will have no doubts at all about which is the main track. Eventually you will cross a stream (the Dour Yvonnic) and climb to the right to meet the D769 after 50m/yds (**2h33min**).

Turn right along the main road and, in seven minutes, you will pass a junction on the left, where the GR380 joins you. (You can follow the waymarks for a while now.) In a further 50m/yds you must turn right, opposite a cinder road on your left, along a tiny waymarked path leading into the wood. The path brings you to a ford across the Dour Yvonnic (but a footbridge on the right will keep your feet dry). The path climbs: in nine minutes, ignore a track on the left. Two minutes later, you come to a junction of tracks. Here follow the waymarks to the right.

Now care is needed once again. Some 70m/yds up the hill, there is a track to the left. All the waymarks point along it. You must ignore it, and carry on up the hill. Your track, too, will bend to the left and, in a further 70m/yds, you reach another fork (**2h55min**). This time you *do* turn left, and you will see that this track is also on a GR route. (The earlier junction was where the GR37 and the GR380 joined.) In five minutes ignore a track on the left; continue to head west. At **3h04min** you will see a picnic area at a road junction, where you turn left. After 100m/yds, turn right along the D769a. Pass the track you took to the Camp d'Artus on the right and, just before the bridge, bear right along the Allée Violette, to walk once more beside the Rivière d'Argent (**3h11min**).

In nine minutes ignore the Sentier des Amoureux on your right; make for the white house ahead, with the 'chaos' to your left. This time do not bear right for La Roche Tremblante, but turn left, up stone steps. At the top, bear left again, walking towards the stream, and cross the bridge. On your left, notice the open-air theatre ('Théâtre de verdure'), but bear right (signposted 'Grotte du Diable'). Do not fail to go down the steps into this cavern. Then, following yellow and white waymarks, squeeze between rocks to emerge above the old mill illustrated on page 13. Follow the path back to the road and join it by the Café du Chaos (**3h28min**). Cross the road, and walk beside the lake, back to your starting point (**3h36min**).

5 MENEZ-HOM

Distance: 21.7km/13.5mi; 4h39min

Grade: fairly strenuous

Equipment: walking boots if wet, otherwise comfortable shoes or trainers, sunhat, suncream, raingear, picnic, water, swimwear (the latter for the main walk or Shorter walk 2), towel

How to get there and return: 🚌 to Pentrez Beach (Quimper to Camaret service). Begin and end the walk at the 2h33min-point. 🚗: If you travel by car, begin at Ste-Marie-du-Ménez-Hom (park in the car park in this hamlet, beside the D887, 11 kilometres from Châteaulin in the direction of Crozon in Finistère) or, alternatively, park at Pentrez Beach and begin there, picking up the main walk at the 2h33min-point.

Shorter walks

1 Ste-Marie-du-Ménez-Hom — Ménez-Hom — St-Nic — Ste-Marie-du-Ménez-Hom (14.3km/8.9mi; 3h30min; fairly strenuous). 🚌 to St-Nic. Walk past the church and take the first tarmac road on your right. Follow the walk from St-Nic to Ste-Marie-du-Ménez-Hom, then return to St-Nic by following directions at the start of the main walk. 🚗 to Ste-Marie, as above. Follow the main walk from the car park at Ste-Marie-du-Ménez Hom as far as St-Nic. Before reaching the church, turn left along a tarmac road. After 300m/yds fork right by the cross, and follow the road for about 1.6km/1mi; you will pass (on your right) the entrance to the football ground, a track, and two roads. You will then have climbed to a substantial track on your right. Turn down this track. In five minutes another track joins you, from the right. This is the junction referred to at the 4h11min-point in the main walk. Keep straight ahead and follow the directions from there.

2 Pentrez Beach — Ménez-Yan — St-Nic — Pentrez Beach (12.3km/7.7mi; 2h30min). 🚌 to Pentrez Beach. 🚗: Park behind Pentrez Beach. Facing the sea, turn left and follow the main walk from the 2h33min-point to the junction beyond Ménez-Yan (the 4h11min-point). Turn left here, instead of following the GR to the right and, in six minutes, you will come to a main road. Turn left and follow it downhill for 2km/1.2mi, until you reach the village of St-Nic. Turn left, pass the church (the 2h13min-point in the main walk), and follow the main walk from there.

There are no real mountains in Brittany. This walk takes you up to one of the highest points in the province — the summit of Ménez-Hom (330m/1100ft). Then you descend to sea level, at the long beach of Pentrez-Plage, before returning to the foot of the hill. For most of its length, your walk follows the route of the Grande Randonnée 37, and you will be able to check your direction by reference to the white and red waymarks.

Start the walk by leaving Ste-Marie car park, to face this church

The church, Ste-Marie-du-Ménez-Hom

with its fine belfry and calvary (if you have time, many of the carvings inside are well worth your attention). Bear right along the D47, in the direction of Trégarven and Dinéault. In **11min** bear left along a tarmac road signposted 'Kernalivet' and, after a little under 200m/yds, leave the road and walk up a well-waymarked track on your left. The track quickly becomes quite overgrown – no more than a path. Nine minutes along, ignore a track on your left. Your track gets wider again, is well surfaced and winds through a wooded region, as it climbs rather reluctantly up the side of Ménez-Hom. 'Ménez' is Breton for a smooth, rounded hill, such as this; a sharp, jagged

utcrop is called a 'roc'h'. These hills may be small today, ut once they were the Himalayas and Andes of their eneration, before erosion reduced them to their present umble size. And if you think that must have taken an wfully long time, you are right. The hills of Lower Brittany re some of the oldest mountains to be found on our lanet, thrust up during the Primary Era, some 600 million ears ago.

At **30min** into the walk (some 17 minutes after starting p this track), you'll see a faint footpath on the left with GR waymark on a tree just after its start. Turn up this ath. In ten minutes you will see another GR waymark

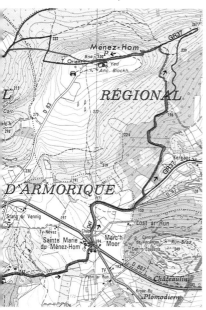

warning you to turn left. You come to a crossing track: turn left and head for the summit of the hill. After a climb of five minutes, you arrive at a second junction, where you again bear left. Five minutes later, ignore two tracks to the left and one to the right; continue to climb towards the summit. As you do so, you pass the remains of old fortifications on your left.

You should be n the summit (**P**8) in **1h**. The next bit is tricky, but you ave the GR waymarks to help you. Look towards the car ark and the hill to its right. Now, if you look further to ne right, you will see a stone on the ground not far away, earing a GR waymark. As you walk towards it, you will ee a path curving away to the right; beside it, there are ill more GR37 waymarks. Of the several paths leading /estwards from the summit, this is the one furthest to the ght, and also the narrowest. There are waymarks every ?w metres/yards at the start. After six minutes the path ppears to go almost vertically downhill. But this steep escent only lasts for a short distance and, in four minutes, you go over a crossing track and along a path opposite well waymarked with red dots. Follow it over open field until, in five minutes, you come to another crossing track here turn left, to reach the main D887 road in three minutes (**1h18min**).

Cross the road and follow a wide gravel track through gorse and heather. In eight minutes pass a track on the left and, four minutes later, arrive at the hamlet of Coatére (**1h30min**). Turn left at the T-junction, along a metalled road, still being led by the GR waymarks; then bear right along a tarred track 50m/yds further on. After the last houses the tarring finishes, and you continue along a lightly-wooded, rough gravel track, enjoying pleasant views. In the next couple of minutes, ignore tracks to the right and then to the left. Seven minutes later, pass the entrance to Trohom farm, after which your track becomes a tarmac road once more. Three minutes along the tarmac turn left at T-junction with a wider road. Ignore the road on your right to Kerroland; you soon pass a water tower on your left. Two minutes beyond the tower, bear right at a junction and, in a further two minutes, come to the junction with the D63 (**1h55min**), by a wooden GR signpost.

Cross the road, and go down a track almost directly opposite, to the right of a farm building. In a few minutes the track becomes a tarmac road. Within 100m/yds, you arrive at a junction, on a bend in the road. The GR37 goes to the right, but you leave it here: follow the road straight ahead. A red and white cross on the telegraph pole tells you that you are no longer on the GR. Ahead you can see the village of St-Nic, which you will reach in five minutes. Turn right at the junction with the D63. Soon you will pass a road on the left. (*Shorter walk 1 turns left here, and Shorter walk 2 rejoins the main walk.*) You reach the church of St-Nic at **2h13min**.

Beyond the church, turn right on the D108, signposted 'Pentrez', and briefly detour along the first track to the right for 100m/yds, to see the 'Feunteun ar Zant', St-Nic' holy well. Then carry on along the D108 for 200m/yds where you fork left for Bernal. Ignore a lane to the left in six minutes and, in another three minutes, enter Pentrez. Again ignoring all side turnings, follow the road down to the sea (**2h33min**). Here, at least during the summer season, you will be able to buy food and refreshments if necessary. (*This beach is the alternative starting point; it is also the starting point for Shorter walk 2.*)

Facing the sea, turn left and walk southwards for ?.5km/1.5mi, behind or along this glorious beach. Some ¦6 minutes later (**3h09min** into the walk), leave the beach ›y steps, cross the road, and turn left (beside a café) along ı minor tarmac road. Since you are now back on the route ›f the GR37, look for the waymark on the telegraph pole. ın 15 minutes go straight over at the crossroads; four ninutes later, turn left along the first track you come to not waymarked). In two minutes the track crosses a brook ınd turns right. Three minutes later, go over a crossing rack, and climb to the farmyard of La Forêt. Bear left across he yard, then turn right at the junction with a tarmac road. ın five minutes you will be at another T-junction in Lesloys. Here turn left and, in 70m/yds, turn right at the junction vith the D63 (**3h43min**). Ignore a track on the left in three ninutes and, in 100m/yds, pass the road to Moulin l'Abbé. ´ou are now back on the waymarked route. In five minutes ırn left on a sandy track (by a wooden GR signpost) and, ın 20m/yds, turn left on joining a tarmac road.

In two minutes pass a road on the left which leads to ›t-Juliau's chapel (which you can see); ignore, too, a road ›n the right. Your climb will be a little steeper now, for he remainder of the walk. In seven minutes (after some ·h walking) you will be at a small crossroads, where you eep straight ahead and pass through the hamlet of Ménez-´an, beyond which the tarred surface ends. Climb through ·ees for six minutes to arrive at a T-junction (**4h11min**). *This is where Shorter walk 1 rejoins the main walk: keep ‹traight ahead. Shorter walk 2 turns left here.)*

Turn right and, in three minutes, bear right at a junction ›f tracks. In a further four minutes, cross over a tarmac ›ad and go up the facing (waymarked) metalled road. ˙here are attractive views over the valley to the right, and ›on the belfry of Ste-Marie's church comes into view ·head. Four minutes along the metalled road, keep right ‹t the fork, and descend to where the tarmac ends. Follow ·e ensuing footpath over a brook and up to a T-junction ·vith a wider track (**4h30min**). Turn left and continue to ·limb, as the track bends first to the left and then to the ·ght. On the skyline the hump of Ménez-Hom can be ·een. One final turn to the left sees you heading for the ·hurch, and the track becomes tarred to return you to the ·ar park in under **4h40min**.

If you began the walk at St-Nic or Pentrez, turn to the ·valking notes on page 65 and carry on until you reach ·our starting point, adjusting times accordingly.

6 IN THE ARRÉE HILLS

See map pages 72-73
Distance: 14.5km/9mi; 3h15min   **Grade:** fairly strenuous

Equipment: walking boots preferably, especially if wet, otherwise comfortable shoes or trainers, sunhat, suncream, raingear, picnic, water

How to get there and return: 🚌 to St-Rivoal, at the heart of the Arrée Hills and the Parc Naturel Régional d'Armorique. It is reached from the D785 Morlaix to Quimper highway by turning west along either the D30 or the D42. There is a large car park in the centre of the village.

Alternative walk: This walk may be combined with Walk 7 (22km/ 13.7mi; about 4h50min; see map pages 72-73). Do this walk first and, at the 2h35min-point, pick up the notes at the 35min-point in Walk 7.

This is a peaceful walk through a very quiet part of Brittany; much of it follows a ridge of the Arrée Hills, often with fine views, sometimes through woodland.

Begin the walk in the car park: face the church, with the *mairie*, village shop and school on your right. Now turn right and walk along the D42, signposted 'Le Faou'. (Since the first 26 minutes of the walk is on the route of the GR37 you have the additional help of the white and red waymarks, the first of which you will see on an electricity pole.) In five minutes the D42 crosses a brook, bends left, and starts to climb. Halfway up the hill there is a timber-yard on the left; a tarmac lane curves behind it. Turn down this lane, bearing right beyond the timber-yard, to walk between fir trees. In **16min** you come to a fork. Do not cross the stream here, but bear right, to walk along the waymarked path beside it. In five minutes the path climbs to the right, away from the stream, eventually emerging on a metalled road, by a bend. Here you leave the GR37 (which goes left), and turn right, climbing uphill. Remain on the tarmac until the top of the hill, where you cross the D42 (**32min**) and keep straight ahead.

Pass the farm buildings of Penn ar Guer, ignoring a road and track on the right, as well as a track on the left. The somewhat overgrown track that you are following is now but a footpath between trees. In two minutes you reach a junction and turn right along the D42. Pass the hamlet of Bodingar and ignore a road on the right. Four minutes later, keep straight ahead along a minor road, when the main road bends left for Ménez-Meur.

The road climbs steadily now for almost 3km/1.8mi; you enjoy splendid views over the valley, as the countryside becomes more and more wild (and the birds more prolific). After half an hour you will be passing an area of gorse and broom on your right, with a wood ahead on your left. Your road also ends some 100m/yds ahead, at

T-junction. At just about the point where the wood begins, on your right, there is a narrow footpath doubling back through the gorse and broom. Turn sharp right here, briefly following the GR380. (At the time of writing, there were orange and white arrows — Petite Randonnée waymarks — painted on the tarmac at the turn-off to this path.) Although it begins as a mere footpath, it quickly widens out to become a respectable track, and you will soon realise that in its day this was an important cart road along the ridge. For a long time the track passes through rough open country that is teeming with birds.

At **1h37min** into the walk you will be standing beneath power cables, and here the GR380 branches off to the left. Continue to follow the track ahead. Some 22 minutes after leaving the GR380 (**2h**), the track enters woodland, by a signpost bearing the legend 'Circuit de Petite Randonnée'. Ignore the tracks that go to the left or right, and head eastwards for another 13 minutes, until you come to a crossing road — the D30. Cross over and carry on along the track opposite, mostly through woodland, in an east-southeasterly direction, still ignoring the one or two tracks going off at right angles. After 22 minutes you reach another road (**2h35min**). (*If you are doing the Alternative walk, cross this road and continue along the track opposite, picking up the notes for Walk 7 at the 35min-point.*)

Turn right down this road. Pass a farm on the left and climb to pass another farm on the right. In 12 minutes turn right again at a crossroads, beside the delightful tiny calvary shown below. Continue climbing for eight minutes. Now the road bends right, as indicated by white chevrons. On the left you will see two tracks: ignore the one running at right angles to the road; take the one going more or less straight ahead. Probably there is a stone surface underneath, but this is now a grassy track. However, since it lies on a Petite Randonnée route, it will probably have been mown.

After 12 minutes turn right along a tarmac road, then go left at the junction with the D42, to arrive back at St-Rivoal in eight minutes (**3h15min**).

You will discover this little calvary above St-Rivoal.

7 MENEZ-MIKEL

Distance: 12.9km/8mi; 2h53min   **Grade:** fairly strenuou

Equipment: walking boots preferably, certainly if wet, otherwise com
fortable shoes or trainers, sunhat, suncream, raingear, picnic, water

How to get there and return: 🚌 to St-Rivoal, at the heart of the Arré
Hills and the Parc Naturel Régional d'Armorique. It is reached from th
D785 Morlaix to Quimper highway by turning west along either th
D30 or the D42. There is a large car park in the centre of the village
Alternatively, leave the D785 some 7km/4.4mi north of Brasparts an
drive up the narrow road to the car park on the summit of Ménez-Mike
Begin the walk at the chapel of St-Michel (1h20min in the main walk

Alternative walk: This walk may be combined with Walk 6 (22km
13.7mi; about 4h50min). Do Walk 6 first and, at the 2h35min-point i
that walk, pick up the notes for this walk (at the 35min-point).

This walk in the Arrée Hills, mostly through forest, lead
you to the tiny chapel of St-Michel atop the highes
hill in Brittany, with views over the desolate marsh an
the Lac de Brennilis, where the river Elez has its source

Starting in the car park at St-Rivoal, turn your back t
the church and walk away from it, up the D30. After
few metres/yards, turn right on the D42 (signposte
'Morlaix'). Almost immediately bear right again, along th
minor road to Bodenna. Part-way up the hill (**6min**), tur
left along a grassy track, climbing between trees. Som
11 minutes later, bear right along the D42. After seve
minutes you reach a crossroads, where you turn left i
front of a quaint little calvary. The road takes you dow

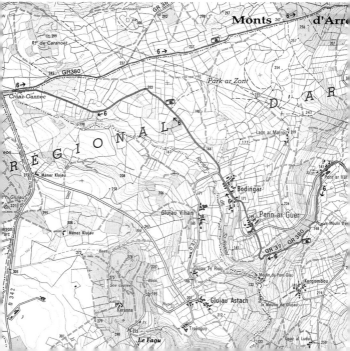

to a valley, past a farm on the left, and climbs out past
another farm on the right. Just beyond this latter farm,
ignore a crossing track and continue to climb for another
00m/yds, until the tarmac ends at a second crossing track.
urn right here; the track is waymarked with an orange
rrow (**35min**). (*If you are doing the Alternative walk, leave
Walk 6 at this point.*)

This track is rough in places and can be quite wet after
ain, so that good boots are recommended. At times, too,
shrinks in width to little more than a footpath. Ignore a
ack on the right (**49min**). Four minutes later, the path
urns right and widens again. There are relay aerials ahead
n your left now and, for the moment, you have reached
e highest part of your climb.

Pass through an area of gorse bushes, between the
erials, and come to a metalled road (D42; **58min**), where
ou turn right. So far the walk has been waymarked with
e yellow and orange signs of the Petite Randonnée. In
ily 20m/yds turn left along a gravel track across open
oorland. After nine minutes along the track, leave it:
rn left on a signposted footpath which leads to the hill
Ménez-Mikel, known in French as 'Mont St-Michel de
rasparts'. On its summit you can see the little chapel of
Michael. If you turn right when you come to the quarry,
ou will pass through a small car park (*an alternative*

The bleak hilltop setting of the Chapelle de St-Michel (Picnic 9)

starting point for the walk. Take the steps up to the chapel shown here (**1h 20min**), from where there are splendid views (**P**9). To the east is a desolate depression at the source of the river Elez. The lake (Lac de Brennilis) is the result of a modern dam. Previously this whole area, known as the Yeun Elez, was marsh. So grim was its reputation that Breton legend held it to be one of the entrances to hell. Standing here on a grey, low-clouded Breton day, that does not seem unreasonable.

Return to the car park and turn left down a tarmac road. After 250m/yds there is a lay-by on the right: here take the narrow footpath to a track some 500m/yds lower down the hill. (Or you can go a little further down the road and turn right along the track itself.) Turn right on the track and, two minutes later, you will arrive at a well-signposted crossing track. Turn right along the GR37 in the direction of St-Rivoal (notice now the white and red waymarks) and walk towards a pylon (**1h38min**).

As before, the track narrows and widens from time to time. In ten minutes ignore a track on the left, and go on to pass through gorse and heather before entering conifer woods. Here the path forks, only to come together again after 200m/yds. Ignore tracks on the left in three minutes and five minutes later. Keep heading west, with the wood becoming increasingly dense. In 11 minutes ignore tracks to the right and then the left.

Ten minutes later emerge from the trees on the left (your path is descending noticeably now). In two minutes you reach the junction with the D30 (**2h22min**). Turn right, following the white and red waymarks, not the orange ones, and walk along this road for 20 minutes — until you come to the first tarred road on the right. Turn here and, in 100m/yds, turn left at a T-junction. Descend quite steeply for five minutes, until you rejoin the D30. Then bear right, cross a stream, and follow the road round and up to St-Rivoal and the car park (**2h53min**).

THROUGH THE VALLEY OF THE ELORN

e photograph page 24

istance: 16.8km/10.5mi; 4h02min   **Grade:** moderate

quipment: walking boots preferably, certainly if wet, otherwise com-
rtable shoes or trainers, sunhat, suncream, raingear, picnic, water

ow to get there and return: ⊞ to Sizun, in the heart of Finistère. Leave
e N12 at Landivisiau and drive 15.5km south on the D30, along the
lley of the river Elorn. There is ample parking space in the village.

ort walk: Circuit of Lake Drennec (7km/4.3mi; 1h30min; easy; equip-
ent as above). ⊞: Drive eastwards from Sizun on the D764 for 0.5km/
3mi, then take the second fork on the right, to Kerféos and Drennec.
llow the country lane for 4km/2.5mi, then turn right in Kerféos. Park
er 0.5km/0.3mi, at Le Drennec. Cross the dam and follow the sign-
sted footpath on the left to circle this man-made lake.

his walk has everything you could ask of a country
walk: woodland, farmland, and Lake Drennec. But
st of all is the gently-flowing river Elorn.

Start the walk in the church square of Sizun, famous
r its parish close. Face the sixteenth-century triumphal
ch (photograph page 24), arguably the finest in Brittany,
d walk to the right of the church, eastwards along the
764. In **3min** turn left along the Rue des Primevères and,
ithin a minute, ignore a street on the left. You have joined
e GR380; its white and red waymarks will help to guide
u for the next two and a quarter hours. In two minutes
ass the *gendarmerie*; in a further four minutes, the tarmac
ds in a gravel track. Follow it through farming country
r 13 minutes, until you arrive at the junction with the
764 (**22min**). Follow the road opposite to the hamlet of
ergleuziou and, after 175m/yds, turn left on another
ack. Six minutes later, turn right along a metalled road
St-Maudez and, after 100m/yds, follow the GR signs
the right, along a gently-ascending gravel track.

Eight minutes along the track (**36min**), go over a tarmac
ad and continue along a track to the left of a quarry.
ur minutes later, at the farm of La Motte, the track forks.
ear right; the track becomes quite overgrown for three
inutes. Then it bends left and widens once more. Five
inutes later you reach a road, where you turn left. After
0m/yds follow the road to the right, round the Penna-
az farm (**48min**). Some 100m/yds further on, keep
raight ahead at a junction of tracks, where the tarmac
ds. After another 250m/yds, bear left at a fork and walk
arallel with the river Elorn for 400m/yds, before bending
ght, to descend through trees into the valley. Care is
eded now. After 150m/yds, you cross a brook. Just
0m/yds beyond the brook, the track divides: turn left
ong a narrow path (waymarked on the trees). In six

minutes the path enters the Kerambloc'h farm (**1h13min**
Cross the farmyard. Do not go down the tarmac road, bu
turn right along a waymarked track, with attractive view
over the Elorn. Continue east down to the river, and follow
the waymarks as the track peters out into a footpath an
climbs north to the hamlet of Kerinizan (**1h29min**).

At the junction with a tarmac road, turn right and follo
the road for nine minutes, as it winds past Creac'h al Liou
until you pass a track on your left. Follow the road uphil
for another 20m/yds, then turn right along a waymarke
track. Beyond a small building the way becomes a foo
path. In two minutes go up steps on your left, then bea
right along another footpath. In three minutes you emerg
on a tarmac road. Turn left and pass in front of a fish farm
Climb to a T-junction (**1h54min**), and turn right to cros
the dam, with Lake Drennec on your left. On the far sid
of the dam, you will see on your left a waymarked footpat
which circles the lake (*Short walk*). You could includ
this circuit at this point (add 1h30min).

Turn right at the end of the dam (signposted 'St-Cadou
and, after 20m/yds, bear left uphill along a track. In anothe
200m/yds turn right along a path which climbs throug
woodland. Follow it for 13 minutes, finally reaching
crossing track. Turn right here, along a good wide track
now you leave the GR380 (**2h17min**). In three minute
keep straight ahead at the junction with a metalled roa

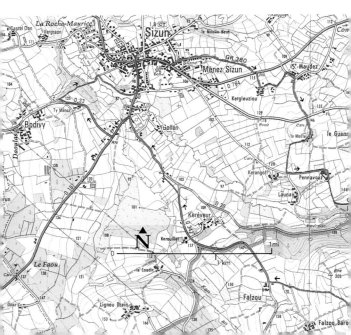

nd, in a further five minutes, when you come to cross-
)ads, again keep straight ahead on track. In six minutes
ou arrive at a T-junction with the D30: turn right. Seven
ninutes later, having passed Lestremelard, bear left along
 road signposted 'Kergreac'h' and 'Falzou'. In three
ninutes turn left uphill along a track (ignoring a path to
e left after 20m/yds). Go under power lines in four
ninutes, then the track bends to the right. Three minutes
ter your way (now only a footpath) forks: bear right.

Three minutes later the path forks again; this time go
ft, to reach a junction with a tarmac road in six minutes.
lere turn right. In three minutes, at the next T-junction,
rn right again. This is the D342 (**3h**), and soon you will
e Sizun straight ahead, 2.6km/1.6mi away. In 13 minutes
gnore roads on the left and then on the right. Six minutes
ter, just short of the next road junction, take the track
) the left, pass a cross, and turn left along the D30. Eight
ninutes later (**3h31min**) you reach the junction with the
)18 on the outskirts of Sizun.

You have a choice here. Either turn right and follow
e main road back into the centre, or turn left along the
)18 for 250m/yds, then take the first road on the right
3h33min). After eight minutes, when the road bends left,
ear right on a sandy track. In 50m/yds you will come to
 stone cross. Notice on your right the entrance to a
/oodland path (which you passed to reach the cross).
etrace your steps and go down it. Go over crossing paths
nd, at the bottom of the hill, cross the Elorn. Turn right
ow and walk beside the river for six minutes, before
rning left up the D18 back to Sizun (**4h02min**).

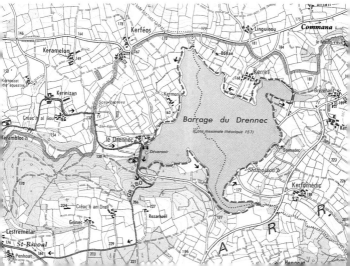

9 THE GRANDE TROMENIE

Distance: 14.8km/9.2mi; 3h35min   **Grade:** moderate

Equipment: walking boots if wet, otherwise comfortable shoes or trainers, sunhat, suncream, raingear, picnic, water

How to get there and return: 🚌 to Locronan. The service between Quimper and Camaret stops at Locronan. 🚗: Locronan is on the D63, 17km northwest of Quimper, in Finistère . There are large car parks at the entrances to the village.

Short walks: This walk, in the shape of a figure 8, divides neatly into two short walks, both beginning in the church square (access as above).
1 Locronan — Plas ar Horn — Locronan (8km/5mi; 2h; grade and equipment as above). Follow the walk below for 2h.
2 Locronan — edge of the Forêt de Névet — Locronan (6.8km/4.2mi; 1h35min; easy; equipment as above). Pick up the main walk at the 2h point and follow it to the end.

A 'Loc' is a holy place. Locronan was the hermitage of an Irish immigrant saint named Ronan. The many fine houses in the village testify to a period when the little town grew rich from the manufacture of sailcloth. Today the village is most famous for its *pardons*, known as 'Troménies'. Every sixth year the Grande Troménie takes place, a procession of some twelve kilometres around the boundary of the former Benedictine priory. (The next will be in 1995.) Since much of the centuries-old route through private land, opened only for the Grande Troménie, one cannot always follow it in its entirety but wherever possible, this walk takes you along the famous pilgrim path.

Start out by facing the church shown opposite: turn left, cross the square, and go down the Rue Moal in the northeast corner. In three minutes turn left at the cross, walk to the right of the Chapelle de Bonne Nouvelle and the fountain of St-Eutrope, then bear right along a footpath. In two minutes cross over the new by-pass and continue along the track opposite, which soon turns left and becomes a footpath. In three minutes, at a crossing track, turn right to follow for the first time part of the route of the Grande Troménie. Ignore the left turn, when the track forks in 10m/yds. Three minutes further on, ignore paths to right and left and, in a further three minutes, you will reach a T-junction (**16min**). Turn right here.

As you pass a house and track on your left, look carefully for a cross on your right, almost obscured by herbage. You will encounter several such crosses in the course of this walk, for they mark the 'stations' or halts for worship made during the pilgrimage. They are dedicated to the patron saints of the neighbouring parishes. This one is to Ste-Anne-la-Palue. Now you leave the Troménie for

78

while, keeping straight ahead to join a tarmac road (**21min**). Turn left. In two minutes pass a road on the left and, after 100m/yds, turn right along a gravel track, to regain the Troménie, by the cross of Troyout, station of Notre Dame de Bonne Nouvelle, whose chapel you passed earlier. In four minutes ignore a track on your right, and then one on the left. Two minutes later, you arrive at the junction with the D63, **31min** into the walk.

Cross the road and carry on along the wide track opposite; in three minutes cross another tarmac road. Walk up the track opposite, beside another cross, the Croaz Ruz, station of St-Milliau. Here you leave the route of the Grande Troménie once more. Your wide, hedged-in track becomes metalled after six minutes and, 100m/yds further on, comes to a road junction, where you turn right. In three minutes pass through the hamlet of Kerarvarn, ignoring tracks to the right and left. In two minutes the road swings left and runs parallel to the D7. Turn left and, in four minutes, pass a road on the left (to 'Bourland').

You now turn left and, unfortunately, you have to walk beside this main road for the next eight minutes. Keep to the left, and take care. After two minutes pass a road on the left and, in a further three minutes, pass another road on the left (signposted 'Bourland'). Some 200m/yds beyond this second road, cross the D7 and turn right up a wide track. Now your steep ascent to the summit of the

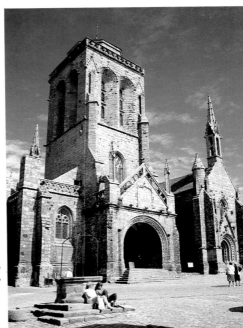

Locronan — the church square

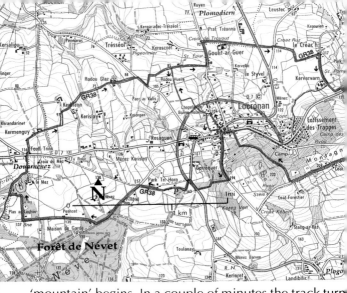

'mountain' begins. In a couple of minutes the track turn
right, in front of a rubbish tip. (There is an inevitabilit
about the way in which these Breton walks, no matte
how lovely, persist in dragging you past the local refus
tip and sewage works.) Turn right where the path forks a
the end of the fence (**1h**). In a couple of minutes the pat
turns left, and rejoins the Troménie, which has come ove
private fields and through the gap in the hedge to you
right. As you climb the slope you will occasionally se
the white and red waymarks of the GR38, which this wal
follows for most of its way. The path runs beside a lov
old stone wall. Do not turn along any of the side path
but walk straight up to the top of the hill.

You may have to squeeze beneath barbed wire a
1h11min and, by **1h17min**, you should reach the summi
having climbed some 150m/yds to attain a height of abou
289m/950ft. You will see a clear path which takes you t
the right, behind and down the side of the chapel, to joi
a tarmac road. This is the Plas ar Horn ('Place of the Horn
see drawing page 8). Here, at the foot of the mountair
the horn of the ox pulling the corpse of St Ronan finall
fell off, having been broken by a furious blow from Kébar
the saint's implacable foe (and wife of his convert). It i
the most sacred spot on the pilgrimage, the station c
St Ronan himself and, as you may have deduced from th
splendid open air stone pulpit, the place where th
pilgrims are regaled with a sermon.

Turn right along the road, pass a track on the left and
in another five minutes, bear left at the fork (in the directio
of Plogonnec). In six minutes ignore a road to the lef

Beyond it a cross marks the station of St Théleau. Five minutes later, you pass a track and, 50m/yds further on, a tarmac drive leading to a *crêperie*. To the right, facing it, is a woodland track, bearing a 'No Entry' sign (for vehicles). Turn down this track (**1h45min**), leaving for a while the pilgrim route. When the track bears left in a minute, ignore the footpath to the right. Two minutes later bear right at a fork. Ignore more footpaths after five minutes and, a minute later, go over a crossing track; then bend left and right and continue ahead. The track is now tarred and, entering Locronan, it joins the D7. Turn left and regain the church square (**2h**).

For the second part of the walk, turn left into the square, walk past the church, and continue south up the Rue St-Maurice. Pass a track on the right, a small cross on the left and, after six minutes, a large house/museum called 'Kerguenolet'. The road enters woodland. In two minutes you leave the road (near a bench), turning down a track on the right into the wood. In two minutes the track divides by a white iron gate. Turn left here and, after 50m/yds, follow it round to the right. In **2h14min** you come to the junction with the D63. Cross the road and turn right, coming to the Locronan by-pass in two minutes. On your left are two tracks. Leave the D63 and turn along the track on the left; the other is private property.

After 100m/yds you come to a three-way junction. Follow the track to the right, ignoring the one to the left and the one through the wood. In two minutes pass a house on the right and, in another three minutes, pass to the left of another large house. Shortly after this the track is metalled. One minute later you turn left at a crossroads.

Soon (**2h26min**) you pass the 'Fer à Cheval' hotel on the left and, three minutes later, a track to the left and a tarmac lane to the right (by a house). Some 200m/yds further along, force yourself to ignore the entrance to the forest of Névet; follow the road to the right. After five minutes you will pass a farm on your left and approach woodland on the right. Four minutes later, turn right down a track, immediately beyond that wood (by electricity poles and a white house). You pass an attractive garden after three minutes, where the track bends to the left; 100m/yds further along, turn right at a T-junction. Now your track is lightly tarred. Two minutes after passing a tennis court, bear left at a T-junction and, after some 200m/yds, arrive at the junction with the D7 (**2h51min**).

Having crossed the road, turn right and, after 10m/yds turn left down a track between houses (signposted 'Ker menguy'). Keep straight ahead at a junction 50m/yds along, following a grassy track (the more used track curls right, between houses). In three minutes bend right, in front of cottages. A minute later, ignore a track to the left and, in another minute, go over a narrow road and continue along grassy track opposite; it runs between trees. Once past a field, the track widens, where it is used more regularly. Soon you must take the track to the right, ignoring the one ahead (which leads to a farm). To your left you can see the village of Plonévez-Porzay (**3h**).

In one minute bear left at the next junction, avoiding the farmyard on your right, and walk downhill. In three minutes the track becomes more overgrown through lack of use, but only for a couple of minutes. Ignore a track to the right leading to another farm, and carry on toward Rodou Glaz farm. When you reach it, ignore another track to the right, and proceed between farm buildings. Keep ahead on a tarmac road for four minutes, then turn right at the road junction (**3h12min**).

Climb for 100m/yds and then, just before the road bends to the left, turn left along a track. In four minutes follow it round to the right and, three minutes later, turn right along an adjacent footpath. This is the footpath on the route of the Troménie that you descended at the very start of the walk. In three minutes ignore the track to the right leading to houses and, after 10m/yds, a path to the left at a well. Keep straight ahead along this sunken path. In three minutes ignore a track to the right but, within 10m/yds, turn left along a footpath. In three minutes cross over the by-pass and go up the path opposite, beside a pole. Bear right in front of the Chapel of Bonne Nouvelle and walk up the track towards two more poles ahead. At the top of the hill you come to a junction. Bear left, at first on a tarmac road, then on cobbles, to see the church square (**3h35min**).

Walk 10 takes you past this dolmen at the Pointe de la Torche. There are probably more visible megalithic monuments in Brittany than anywhere else in the world.

See photograph opposite

Distance: 16.5km/10.2mi; 4h   **Grade:** easy

Equipment: comfortable shoes or trainers, sunhat, suncream, raingear, picnic, water, swimwear, towel

How to get there and return: 🚌 to St-Guénolé from Quimper. From the bus stop in St-Guénolé, follow the street signposted 'Musée', which runs northwest parallel with the coast, until you come to the Museum of Prehistory. (Before leaving the village you will probably want to look at its famous sea-swept rocks; from there, it is just over 1km to the museum.) 🚗: Take the D785 southwest from Quimper to Penmarc'h in southern Finistère. Fork right on the D53 on the outskirts of Penmarc'h or St-Guénolé and, in about 1.75km, turn right to the 'Musée de Pré-histoire/Porz Carn'. Or follow Car tour 3 on page 28 and approach via the d'Eckmühl Lighthouse. Park opposite the museum.

Short walk: Penmarc'h — Pointe de la Torche — Penmarc'h (10.5km/6.5mi; 2h20min; grade, equipment, access as above). Follow the main walk to the Pointe de la Torche, then turn round and follow the road inland straight ahead for almost 2km/1.2mi. Turn right along the road to 'Porstidord' and continue the main walk from the 2h38min-point.

This walk follows an exhilarating, sea-washed beach (one of the longest in Europe), then it turns inland to pass a remarkable church and an even more remarkable calvary, as well as a number of megalithic monuments.

Begin the walk at the Museum of Prehistory: walk down to the beach and turn right. This beach is Porz Carn (**P**10), which you will follow for 2.2km — as far as the Pointe de la Torche headland. Be warned: bathing is forbidden all along this coast, on account of the strong currents. In **5min** you pass a telecommunications tower on your right; straight ahead and inland you can see the distant spire of the church of Notre-Dame de Tronoan. After **30min** you come to the end of this glorious beach, and a footbridge helps you ascend to the Pointe de la Torche promontory. Turn left and walk to its end, passing an old blockhouse and going up steps to the small dolmen shown opposite.

On leaving the promontory, bear left to continue along the beach (*or, if you are doing the Short walk, keep straight along the road*). Now the Plage de Tronoan (or 'Tronoën') stretches before you for an unbroken 12km/7.4mi. After 26 minutes you approach a concrete blockhouse. Just before reaching it, you will see a gap in the dunes on your right (beside a flag-pole). Turn up this gap, pass a car park, and continue along a metalled road. In 20 minutes you reach the chapel of Our Lady of Tronoan. It is a remarkable building to find in this remote windswept spot. Even more remarkable is the magnificent calvary, much worn and eroded: the oldest of the Breton calvaries, it was the inspiration for all the others, because during the Middle Ages

83

this part of 'Ar Mor' was the most prosperous in all Brittany

When you leave the church (**1h45min**), turn right, away from the bar, and follow the road in the direction of the Pointe de la Torche. In four minutes pass a track on the right and a house on the left. After another three minutes the road goes through a line of trees, beyond which you take the road on the left and pass to the left of a small factory. Five minutes later, go over a crossing track, then pass another track on the left after 30m/yds. Look over to your right now (**2h**): across the field, you will see a tall menhir (if the crop is low enough). Pass another track on the left in four minutes and, three minutes later, enter the hamlet of Beuzec. Follow the road to the right, round the chapel, ignoring the two roads on the left. After 100m/yds keep left at the fork, for Kerugou. In three minutes, just before a farm on your left, there is another dolmen on

your right, in a field (**2h15min**). Some 30m/yds further on, turn right along a short track; then continue on a tarred road, ignoring a track on the right. But a minute later, go right on another track. Eight minutes along it, go left at a T-junction and walk between houses; then pass a road on the left. Turn right at the next T-junction, seven minutes along, and continue along a busier road (fortunately with wide grass verges) for eight minutes, passing a track to the left in five minutes and one to the right three minutes later. At **2h38min** you come to a junction. Turn left for Porstidord. *(The Short walk rejoins the main walk here.)*

In two minutes notice a small lichen-covered menhir on your right, dwarfed by an electricity pylon. Soon after passing a campsite, you come to riding stables on your right and a track leading to Kermeil and the Pointe de la Torche. Opposite these there is a footpath: turn left down it and, after crossing a stream, continue to the left. In three minutes turn right along a wide track (by a cottage). Then bear left along a crossing track, in front of the chapel of La Madeleine. Beyond the chapel, turn right on a tarmac road and go straight ahead at crossroads, along the Rue de la Madeleine. In three minutes turn right on the Rue des Menhirs. Eight minutes later, ignore a road on the right, then the Rue de Ménez-Gad on the left. A minute later turn left at the T-junction. Ahead the spires and tower of Penmarc'h church come into view. Pass the Rue des Pratandoc on left. After 50m/yds take the next turning right, the Rue des Sarcelles. This is the hamlet of Méjou Braz (**3h10min**).

In four minutes turn right at the first crossroads (Route de Kerloc'h), to cross a partially-drained marsh, the Marais de Lescors. Some 27 minutes later (**3h41min**), cross a road and go straight ahead on a track (to the left of a bungalow). The path bears left and runs beside a hedge, before coming to a wide track. Turn left and soon cross a tarmac road. Continue on a sandy path which bears left, towards a telecommunications tower. In three minutes go over a crossing path and, in a further three minutes, join a wider track by a metal pole. Walk towards the right of a row of trees, heading for the tower. Beyond the trees a path takes you to the dunes and, in five minutes, you pass between the tower and the dunes. Enter a parking area and turn right to the beach, then go left to the museum (**4h**).

11 POINTE DU RAZ

Distance: 14.4km/9mi; 3h50min

Grade: fairly strenuous, demanding a head for heights and reasonable agility for the cliffside section

Equipment: walking boots if wet, otherwise comfortable shoes or trainers, sunhat, suncream, raingear, picnic, water, swimwear (but check that bathing is permitted), towel

How to get there and return: 🚌 to the Pointe du Raz from Quimper. 🚗: drive westwards from Quimper to the Pointe du Raz, at the very end of the D784. There is extensive pay car parking.

Short walk: Pointe du Raz — Baie des Trépassés — Pointe du Raz (7.5km/4.7mi; 2h; grade, equipment, access as for the main walk). Follow the main walk until, halfway across the Baie des Trépassés, you are opposite the hotel (1h11min). Turn right and leave the beach. Pass by the hotel and, on coming to a tarmac road, turn right. Now pick up the notes for the main walk again, from the 3h-point.

The Pointe du Raz is Cornouaille's 'Land's End'. It is every bit as commercialised as Cornwall's, even possessing a *cité commerciale*. It is still a 'must' for tourists, however, and this walk will quickly take you away from the majority of your fellow visitors, along a most impressive coast. Of all the walks in the book, this one should appeal most to bird lovers who, if they have come by car, might well consider returning on the D7, and visiting the Cap Sizun bird sanctuary.

To begin the walk, leave the car park and head westwards past the radar station and Godepski's statue to Notre Dame des Naufrages ('Our Lady of Shipwrecks'). One wonders what exactly the Bretons of old would have considered the Virgin's role to be in relation to shipwrecks, given that the local populace depended on them for a large part of its livelihood. Indeed for centuries this was notorious as a wreckers' coast.

St-They's chapel, near the Pointe du Van

You will no doubt wish to explore the rocky cape. Having done so, stand facing the statue and walk to the left of the promontory. Time your departure from here at about **10min**. When you reach the edge of the cliff, turn right and follow the coastline away from the cape. There are many paths from which to choose. The more nervous or less agile should stay on the uppermost path, as indeed should everyone if the weather is stormy; otherwise the paths partway down the cliff are more interesting. In the spring these rocks are crowded with nesting gulls and shags. Wheatears are common, you will never be out of earshot of a skylark, while these shores of Finistère are one place where you are as likely to see a cuckoo as hear one (more often than not being chased by some small bird). If you have picked the right path (ie, part way down the cliff), at **19 min** you will come to a cave offering picnic shelter in the event of rain.

Having rounded one craggy inlet after another, in **33min** you should be about level with a white building (an hotel). Here the path forks, with a track diverging to the right and leading to the village of Lescoff. Your way is to the left, to continue along the cliff-top. In four minutes take the path that winds fairly steeply down the cliff; continue halfway down, on what is basically a good path, although in places quite badly eroded.

At **1h06min** the path begins to descend to the beach, passing some old fortified positions, as you set foot on the sand and walk across the Baie des Trépassés ('Dead Men's Beach'). Legend has it that the macabre name commemorates the drowned victims of those shipwrecks mentioned earlier, whose bodies were washed ashore here. (*The Short walk turns right when you are level with the hotel — about halfway across the bay or in* **1h11min**.)

At the far side of the bay (**1h16min**), climb up the cliff and follow the path, to resume your walk round the coast. In ten minutes turn left on a tarmac road and, at the end of the promontory of Le Vorlenn, turn right, climb up, and continue your walk along the cliff path. Beyond Le Vorlenn there are a couple of quite steep little valleys. If they are too steep for you, bear right and walk round the heads of them, before returning to the cliff-edge. This open grassy flat region offers several delightful picnic spots.

In **1h46min** the cliff-top chapel of St-They, shown opposite, comes into view. As you walk towards it, keep your eyes open for the holy well. Throughout Brittany you will find holy wells in the vicinity of quite remote chapels.

It is the wells that give the sites their sanctity, and they were objects of worship long before the coming of Christianity. The chapels were an attempt by the church to harness the ancient Bretons' devotion to a more acceptable faith.

After passing the chapel (**1h53min**) ignore a dirt road to the right; carry on beside the coast, alongside numerous tiny islets thronged with gulls. In nine minutes (**2h02min**) you arrive at the Pointe du Van ... far less crowded than the Pointe du Raz. A telescope is provided here.

Your path turns eastward now, still beside the sea, until you come to a region of dry-stone walled fields (**2h16min**). Here the way forks, with a wide path bearing right. However, both paths meet up again shortly, so you could take either. In four minutes you go through an area of gorse for some 100m/yds, then bear right to approach a dry-stone wall and a track, some 50m/yds to the left of houses. Turn right along the track, and walk past the houses of Keriolet, ignoring a path to the left. Go by the farm drive, and immediately fork left. At **2h29min** you will be at a crossroads with a tarred road. Go straight over and continue on a tarmac road, with an old windmill on your right. Four minutes later, reach the D7 and turn left.

Three minutes along the road, take the first road on the right, opposite a metal cross supported by a stone pillar. Two minutes later, turn left at the next junction. Pass through the farm of Kerléo, ignore a track on the left and, at **2h41min**, turn right down a tree-lined gravel track. After 50m/yds bear left at the junction and, in a further 20m/yds, bear right at the next junction. Proceed downhill through a delightful wooded region for three minutes, until you come to another fork. Bear right, and continue to descend, with a brook beyond the trees to your right.

At **2h50min** you leave the wood and pass a farm, now on tarmac, heading for the lake ahead (Etang de Laoual); ignore a track on the left and a road on the right. Before he built Quimper, King Gradlon ruled from Ys, the most beautiful city in all the world. Unfortunately it lay below the level of the surrounding sea, which was kept at bay by gates. One day his daughter Dahut, in order to please her lover (who, it transpired, was the Devil himself, no less) stole the silver key and opened the gates. Ys disappeared beneath the waters. Most legends locate the vanished city in Douarnenez Bay, but local people maintain that Ys lies submerged beneath this lake.

At the T-junction, turn right and, in five minutes, pass

a road on your right. At **3h** bear left behind the Baie des Trépassés. (*Here the Short walk rejoins the main walk.*) Pass the hotel named after the bay and, in three minutes, where the road bends left inland, fork right up a path, to climb towards the village of Lescoff. After two minutes turn right at the T-junction with a narrow road, ignore a track descending on your right, and follow the road towards houses. After 20m/yds leave the road, to follow a track going uphill to the left. When you reach the outskirts of Lescoff, the track becomes metalled. Near the top of the hill, there is a road on the left, and a track opposite on the right, near electricity poles. Turn right along that track, initially following the line of the electricity cables. The track narrows to a good footpath and, after four minutes, passes more old gun emplacements.

In ten minutes (**3h25min**) the path swings left and forks. Go left and, in three minutes, bear left on a good gravel track. Two minutes later cross the tarmac road to the car park and go down the track opposite. Over the field, on your left, there are now some houses. After just a minute, ignore a track on the right and, in a further minute, another on the left. Carry on along this wide track for eight minutes, until it bends inland towards the radar station and brings you back to the car park and bus stop (**3h50min**).

12 IN GAUGUIN'S FOOTSTEPS

Distance: 11km/6.8mi; 2h40min   **Grade:** easy

Equipment: walking boots if wet, otherwise comfortable shoes or trainers, sunhat, suncream, raingear, picnic, water

How to get there and return: 🚌 to Pont-Aven from Quimper, Concarneau, or Quimperlé. 🚗: to Pont-Aven in south-east Finistère, between Concarneau and Quimperlé. Park in the main square or by the river.

Read the notes about Pont-Aven on pages 27 and 28 before setting out on this walk; it will 'paint the scene' and tell you more about Gauguin and his contemporaries.

In the centre of the village a bridge (*pont*) crosses the river Aven. **Begin the walk** on the east bank, by the tourist office in the Place de l'Hôtel-de-Ville. Cross the bridge to the west bank and turn right. Walk some 50m/yds up the Rue Emile Bernard, then take the first turning on the right, in front of the large wall map displaying local walks. Bear right towards the river once more, and go over the footbridge to a little island. Ignoring the bridge that completes the river crossing, turn left and walk along this pretty island as far as the next footbridge. Now turn left, following signs for the 'Bois d'Amour'. On reaching the road, turn right and climb to a T-junction.

Cross over the road and pass between stone gateposts, to enter the Bois d'Amour ('Love's Wood'), made famous by the painters of Pont-Aven. Fork right (ignore the blue waymarks) and take the path down to the river, which soon begins to bend to the right. Here Paul Sérusier received a lesson in painting from Gauguin and painted (on a cigar box!) his landscape of the Bois d'Amour that became known as 'The Talisman'. Ahead is the Moulin Neuf, which you can see in that extraordinary picture.

In another 10 minutes the river bends once more to the right; here Emile Bernard painted his sister Madeleine lying on the grass beneath the trees. In those days no unsightly factories disfigured the right bank; there were only graceful watermills. You arrive at a bridge and road junction in **20min**. Ignore the waymarked path forking uphill to the left, and continue along the track, to the left of a sewage works. Soon you are walking between two arms of the river. Five minutes later ignore the path to the left; continue to follow the river for another eight minutes. At this point the path begins to bend to the left, away from the river.

After a few metres/yards the path forks (**35min**). Taking the path to the left, leave the river and climb uphill through the trees, along what becomes a fairly wide footpath. After three minutes, the path forks: again keep left. Six minutes later, the path swings left round the head of a little valley.

Ignore the track coming from the right; carry on downhill, along the far side of the valley, on the wide (possibly muddy) woodland track. Ten minutes beyond that junction, you will come to another: turn left again and follow the track round to the left, climbing to the accompaniment of (caged) barking dogs, towards the Château du Plessis. Turn right by the wrought iron railings which front this fine manor house, along a wide tree-lined tarmac drive (**1h**). After 500m/yds turn left, in front of the farm of Quistilliou. Three minutes later, bear right at a Y-junction for the Chapelle de Trémalo. You reach this early 16th-century chapel in three minutes. It is attractive enough, but what draws art lovers to this place hangs within — the large painted wooden crucifix which was the inspiration for Gauguin's 'Yellow Christ'.

Beyond the chapel (**1h12min**) turn right along another tree-lined track and, in three minutes, turn left along a wide track. In six minutes you come to a crossing of tracks and a road. Keep straight ahead here, on a sunken track between trees. In two minutes cross a road, then continue along a similar track ahead. Pass a farm on the left and, at the junction with the D24 (**1h27min**), cross over. Turn right; then, after 40m/yds, turn left along a tarmac road. In four minutes you arrive at a large square/car park. This is Nizon. Turn right along a road next to an oak tree and seat and, at the next T-junction, turn left. You come to the parish church (with Guével's notable stained glass) and a very old calvary, whose composition again moved Gauguin, this time to paint his 'Green Christ' (**1h35min**).

Cross the D77, on your left, and walk down the Rue des Grandes Chênes opposite, back to the square. Then continue straight ahead, walking down the right-hand side of the square, to leave Nizon by the road opposite. In four minutes ignore the road on your left; three minutes later

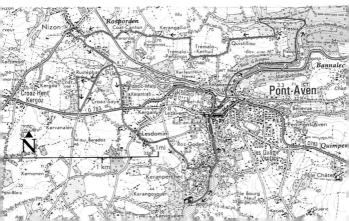

Ghostly ruins: Château de Rustéphan

you come to a cross-roads. Turn right here, passing a factory on your left. In a further three minutes turn right along a tarmac lane. At the end of this lane there are farm buildings: 20m/yds before them, take a woodland track to your left and, on your right, you will see amongst the trees the haunted ruins of Jean du Faou's 15th-century castle of Rustéphan, shown here (**1h45min**).

About 100m/yds along, the track forks. Ignore the track to the right, and walk for about 10m/yds to the left, to where the track forks again. Ignore the track which goes off to the left and passes through a hedge to enter a field. Instead, keep straight ahead along a path down the middle of a somewhat overgrown track which, in its heyday, was the castle drive. Its entrance may be barred against cattle with wire. Follow this path for four minutes, then turn left, when you arrive at a tarmac road. After 350m/yds, pass the end of the the lane leading up to Rustéphan; now retrace your steps to the crossroads and turn right. Cross a stream, pass the factory entrance, and climb to pass the hamlet of Kerentreh on your left. Seven minutes beyond the crossroads, you reach the D783 (**2h05min**). Cross it and go down the track opposite. Bear left in two minutes, along a tarmac road. In a further two minutes, keep straight ahead at the crossroads, along a lightly-tarred road. Ignore the track to the right four minutes along but, two minutes later, at yet another crossroads, turn right. Follow the road as it bends left (in six minutes) and then sharp right downhill (two minutes later). In a few metres/yards, cross a road junction and go down steps opposite (following a blue arrow), to reach the Aven once more (**2h25min**).

Turn right, and follow the river as far as the car park (and another sewage works), for a lovely view of the river. If you climb up the steps in the right-hand corner of the car park and follow the footpath up through the wood, an even finer view is had from the meadow above. Then retrace your steps beside the river, passing Botrel's Square on your left and some beautifully-decorated mills on your right. When you are back at the bridge, turn right and cross over to the Place de l'Hôtel-de-Ville (**2h40min**).

13 THE MENHIRS OF CARNAC

See also photograph page 20
Distance: 14.5km/9mi; 3h10min   **Grade:** easy
Equipment: comfortable shoes or trainers, sunhat, suncream, raingear, picnic, water, swimwear, towel, *torch*
How to get there and return: 🚌 to Carnac (ville) from Vannes, Auray or Quiberon. 🚗: to Carnac town (ie, not Carnac Plage). There is a car park some 200m/yds west of the parish church, off the rue St-Cornély (D781), by the bus stop, which is where the walk starts.

I t would be as unthinkable to visit Brittany without seeing the alignments of Carnac as to visit Egypt and not see the pyramids. The megaliths are not Carnac's only attraction for visitors, however, and this walk also gives you the chance to appreciate its magnificent bathing beach.

Begin at the bus stop/car park: walk west, away from the town centre. In 100m/yds turn up the first road on the right, signposted 'Les Alignements'. Pass a sports ground on your left and, in **9min**, the road swings round to the right. If you keep straight ahead now and enter the hamlet of Le Ménec, you will see that it is partly surrounded by a splendid cromlech, or semicircle of 70 standing stones (menhirs). Turn right towards the lines of stones ahead, for you have reached one of the archaeological wonders of the world, the Alignements du Ménec. Before you 1,099 menhirs, arranged in 11 lines, stretch for over a kilometre. As you will discover, the most splendid stones are here at the start. Walk now along the lines of stones, parallel with the road.

In six minutes cross a tarmac road and carry on along a path opposite: it takes you to the far left-hand corner of the field, where you join a narrow road (by a tennis court). Bear right and, after 50m/yds, cross a main road; continue along a path opposite. It runs between lines of stones, in the direction of a wood. After 20m/yds fork right, and then continue beside the road for three minutes (ignoring a track on the left), until you are able to leave it in favour of a little woodland path on the left, parallel with the road.

Soon you cross a car park and reach more menhirs (**30min**). These are the Alignements de Kermario (photograph page 96), a further 982 stones, laid out in 10 lines

The 2,700 large stones at Carnac, arranged in parallel lines that stretch for 4 kilometres/2.5 miles, are world famous. Although the most impressive of the neolithic monuments of the region, the alignments are far from being the only ones, for the whole coastline from Vannes to Lorient is a vast open-air museum of Stone Age culture, where menhirs, dolmens and tumuli seem to exist round every corner.

which stretch for another kilometre. As before, the largest are to be found at this end. In four minutes you cross a track by a *crêperie* and shop and, three minutes later, fork right on approaching a wood. Pass a small tower on the left and keep on between stones, in a field dominated by asphodel. Finally, entering woodland, you arrive at a small lake. The path turns right to run beside the lake and back to the road once more. Turn left and, beyond the lake, follow another path through lines of stones. After nearly **50min** the second alignment ends, in front of gorse bushes and more woodland. Bear right and rejoin the road. Turn left and continue in the same direction.

Walk beside the road now, through a region of gorse and trees, passing a lane on the right to the Tumulus de Kercado and two woodland paths on the left. The road goes downhill and bends to the left. At the bottom of the hill turn left on a track signposted 'Le Géant et Le Quadrilatère du Manio'. On your right are riding stables. Ignore a path on the left opposite the stables but, four minutes later, turn left along a track signposted 'Quadrilatère du Manio'. After 200m/yds you reach the lofty menhir known as 'The Giant' (photograph page 20) and the interesting structure called the 'Quadrilateral', a rectangular en-

closure surrounded by a wall of single megaliths (**1h**).

Return now along the path and turn right at the junction of tracks, to pass once again by the riding stables. When you come to the tarmac road, cross over and go down the track opposite, into the wood. (However, before doing so, those who are not sated with megaliths may want to view the third and last of the Carnac lines, the Alignements de Kerlescan, another 540 menhirs. They begin at the top of the hill. Then return to this path to continue the walk.)

After 50m/yds ignore a path on the left; then, after a few more metres/yards, look out for a pool, also on the left, and holy well. You pass dwellings on the left and, in six minutes, come to the Château de Kercado (**1h19min**). Cross the tarmac drive to a car park on your left. Cross the car park between the château and barns, following signs for the tumulus. The site entrance is in the far right-hand corner. It is here that you will find your torch handy.

After visiting the tumulus, return to the track and turn left, to continue in the same direction as before. Ignore a track to the left, as you circle the estate and head southwards. Pass three more tracks on the left before coming on to tarmac, as you pass through the hamlet of Kerousse. In three minutes walk straight through the hamlet of Kervinio (**1h30min**), ignoring two roads on the left. Notice another sacred fountain, also on the left, before finally turning right at the junction with the D781.

The road borders marshland, the Marais de Kerdual. Follow it for five minutes, crossing a stream halfway along, by which time you will have reached the entrance to the Domaine du Kerdual on your right (**1h41min**). Turn left, cross to the opposite side of the road, and go down a track along the causeway, soon passing a ruined building. The track narrows to a footpath as you pass a lake on the left and another ruin. After nine minutes, you have crossed the marsh, and you come to a crossing path. Turn right. After 10m/yds, ignore a path on the right. There are many paths around you now, but follow the widest of them, initially going towards a housing development. There is a fairly open field on your left and, when you come to bushes, you will see that the path divides. One fork carries on towards the buildings; the other goes left, following the line of the gorse bushes. That is your way. Walk southwards, parallel with the houses, ignoring a path on the left. But, two minutes later, bear left at a junction, along an ever-widening path. A minute later, ignore a path on the right, as you pass through a tree-shaded picnic area.

The Alignements de Kermario at Carnac disappear into the distance.

You arrive at a main road, the D186 (**1h57min**). Turn right briefly, then cross the road and walk down to the beach. This is the Plage du Men-Du. Turn right and walk along the beach for a quarter of an hour, amusing yourself with watching the sand pipers. Rejoin the road at the end of the beach and turn left. Pass the tennis club, and follow the Avenue d'Orient round to the right, into the Boulevard de la Plage. Bear left now and cross a car park, to go onto the beach again. This is Carnac's Grande Plage, one of the finest bathing beaches in France. You may have found the going a little soft on Men-Du, but the sand here is firm and easy to walk on. It takes 23 minutes to reach the other side of the bay (**2h42min**). When you do so, leave the beach by the port and turn right along the Avenue de l'Atlantique, following the sign 'Parc à Huîtres du Pô'. Oysters (*huîtres*) are farmed all along this coast. You will see the beds on your left.

In nine minutes ignore a road on the left, and keep straight ahead uphill at the roundabout, passing the Armorique Hotel. In six minutes ignore another road on the left, and follow 'Centre Ville' past the post office. Ignore more side roads as you climb past yet another holy well, towards the steeple of the parish church. Twenty minutes after leaving the beach you reach the church, dedicated to St Cornély, patron of horned cattle. Walk round it so that you see the north porch, then continue westwards along the Rue St-Cornély. In three minutes you will be back at the bus stop and car park (**3h10min**).

4 JOSSELIN CASTLE AND THE SEDON VALLEY

Distance: 16.5km/10.2mi; 3h16min   **Grade:** easy

Equipment: walking boots if wet, otherwise comfortable shoes or trainers, sunhat, suncream, raingear, picnic, water

How to get there and return: 🚌 to Josselin. The Rennes to Pontivy and Rennes to Ploërmel services both call at Josselin. 🚗: Josselin is in Morbihan, 72km west of Rennes on the N24. Coming from the west, drive between the castle and the river. There is parking by the river where the road bends to follow the wall of the castle, or carry on to the next T-junction, where another car park (Parking d'Aiguillon) faces you. Coming from the east, there is a car park on your right (Parking d'Aiguillon) at the bottom of the hill as you enter the town, just at the point where you first draw level with the castle wall.

Short walk: Josselin — Le Val au Houx — Josselin (8.8km/5.5mi; 1h40min; grade, equipment, access as above). Follow the main walk for 40 minutes, then turn right along the track, before crossing the stream. Follow the track uphill beside a wood for six minutes, and rejoin the main walk at the 2h26min-point.

R oi ne puis, prince ne daigne, Rohan suis' ('I cannot be king, I scorn to be a prince, I am a Rohan'). Such was the proud boast of the first family of Brittany, whose castle has brought fame and tourists to Josselin. But when you have done with castle and town, turn your back on them and follow this walk deep into the vale of the river Sedon, where you will find almost total solitude.

Start the walk at the Parking d'Aiguillon (see above). At the rear of this car park is the sacred fountain of Notre-Dame-du-Roncier ('Our Lady of the Brambles'; *P*17), which you may like to visit before setting off. The first few metres are on the route of the GR37, and you will notice its white and red waymarks. Head for the river, down the street to the left of the castle. But bear left almost at once, by what remains of a small calvary. As the street climbs, look to your right over the castle wall, where the delight-fully-sculpted façade contrasts markedly with the stern fortifications overlooking the river. Follow the street as it bends left; then bear right and go down steps beside another well. Walk across the car park opposite, to the towpath of the river Oust.

Turn left now (**5min**) and, leaving the GR37, walk along the towpath, away from the town, with the river on your right. The canal-side walks are some of the prettiest in Brittany, and this one is no exception. In one minute pass a dam and lock and, in ten minutes, a beautiful classical house. In a further six minutes, the river divides round an island, and you pass the charmingly-kept lock of St-Jouan. Cross a small road leading over a bridge to the island, and keep on beside the river for another two minutes, until you come to an iron bridge. Leave the canal here by crossing over this bridge (**28min**). Beyond the bridge follow a track to the D4, cross it, and go up the D12 opposite, signposted 'Guégon'. After 200m/yds, turn left for Morhan. Cross a stream and, when the road forks (by a little, almost hidden, stone cross), bear right (**38min**). Pass a track on the right in two minutes. (*But bear right on this track, if you are doing the Short walk.*)

Just beyond this right-hand fork you cross a stream. Two minutes later, turn right along the next track. The river Sedon was formerly lined with watermills; after five minutes you pass one of them, and you will pass several others during this walk. In a further two minutes, turn right at a junction, along a track surfaced with the red shale-like stone you met on the towpath. After seven minutes of winding below trees, the red surface ends, and soon you reach a T-junction with a tarred road (**57min**). Turn left here, to climb away from the river. The road bends sharply to the right and, 200m/yds beyond the junction, begins to bend to the left. A path leaves the road here, to the right; woods run to the left of it, and a meadow is on the right. Take this path and, when it forks in three minutes, go right, downhill.

In five minutes, keep straight ahead at a crossing track and descend close to the river once more. The track times now narrows to a footpath and, across the river, the rocky cliff of the Moto Gross rears up. Ignore a track going uphill on your left. Four minutes later you arrive at a tarmac road (**1h11min**). Turn right and continue along the road initially in much the same southwesterly direction. In a minute ignore a road on the left.

The road swings west and crosses a stream. Continue beside the Sedon and, in three minutes, keep right, where a road joins you from the left. Ignore a red-surfaced track on the left, pass an old mill, and cross the river. Ignore another track on the left; remain on the metalled road it bends eastward, climbing steadily. At **1h30min** pass a path on the right going down through the wood. Three minutes later, as the road doubles back sharply to the left fork right. After 20m/yds, ignore the track that forks left keep ahead on a narrow road (little more than a rough tarred track) that descends to yet another old mill, the Moulin de Roxa (**1h37min**).

Beyond the mill the road deteriorates and runs at the foot of the Moto Gross, beside a meadow. In four minutes you pass a footpath on the left. Soon the track bends left

The fountain of St Anthony (St-Antoine)

nd starts to climb. In another four minutes you come to a T-junction with a good gravel track. Turn left, nd keep climbing for three minutes, to pass through the farm of Le Bot (notice, 50m/yds on our left, a little stone cross). On leaving the farm cross a road and go down the track opposite. The massive buildings ahead belong to the *porcherie* (pig farm) of La Ville Denoual. In three minutes turn right at the next junction and go quite steeply downhill. The track is very well paved, and the reason for this soon becomes apparent. After descending for four minutes, you see rose bushes and flowering shrubs on your right. Follow the path between the shrubs to the fountain of St Anthony, shown above. Beside it is a brook and, just beyond it, a small lake. The track curls round the lake (**2h**) and climbs to a junction with three roads. Take the middle one, opposite, to pass the chapel of St Anthony (St-Antoine). Four minutes later pass the *porcherie* of Trévenaleuc and a number of old cottages and farms, with the surface underfoot gradually deteriorating.

At **2h09min** ignore a track on the left but, two minutes later, turn down a wide track on the right, just before reaching the old farm buildings of Trévenalay. You descend into the valley of the Sedon once more. Ignoring a track on the left into a field, go down to the bottom of the valley, follow the track round to the left, and ignore a path on the right going to the river. For six minutes the track follows the course of the river, with water meadows to the right and woods to the left. Then it seems to fork. Walk to the left, climbing steeply through the trees, as the track narrows to footpath beside a small valley on your right. In four minutes you emerge from the wood and join a red-surfaced track (**2h26min**). Turn left. (*The Short walk rejoins the main walk here.*)

After a minute turn right, when you join a tarmac road (on a bend). Pass the farm of La Ville Jamin. The road bends left and right and then, in three minutes, it crosses a brook and swings right once more, to join the D123 (**2h33min**). Turn right. With woods falling away to the brook, make your way to Le Val au Houx (**2h37min**). This farm is something special; very old, the buildings are a mixture of classical and mediaeval Gothic. After passing it, turn left up the narrow lane signposted 'Gloret'. Beyond Gloret the lane swings right, but bear left here, on a wide gravel track heading northwest, parallel with the D4 (which lies 250m/yds to the east). Ahead, slightly to the right, is the spire of the church of Notre-Dame-du-Roncier in Josselin. Ignore a track on the left, four minutes along, and continue to climb through arable fields along this straight track for nine minutes more.

You reach the hamlet of La Ville Gourdan (**2h53min**). On tarmac now, fork right in two minutes and, very soon, turn right again at a T-junction. Pass between old houses and descend (after 200m/yds) to a T-junction with the D4. Turn left and, after 100m/yds, bear right at the next road junction. Continue to descend towards the river Oust (**3h**).

After 150m/yds turn left along a park path which runs under trees above the river, ignoring a path on the left four minutes along. Three minutes later you will see Josselin Castle across the river. Do not take the path down right to the river, but continue ahead to the main road. Turn right and follow the D4 across the bridge, from where you will get your best view of the imposing wall of the castle. Beyond the bridge, turn right and follow the road in front of the castle and then round to the left, to return to the car park (**3h16min**).

Distance: 20km/12.4mi; 4h35min   **Grade:** fairly strenuous

Equipment: walking boots if wet, otherwise comfortable shoes or trainers, sunhat, suncream, raingear, picnic, water

How to get there and return: 🚌 to Le Faouët. Unfortunately the service between Lorient and Le Faouët is meagre and unlikely to be of much use to walkers, since it tends to take you from Le Faouët to Lorient in the morning and bring you back in the afternoon — the reverse of what you need. 🚗: Le Faouët is a small town in Morbihan, 35km north of Lorient on the D769. Park in the market square in the town centre.

Shorter walk: Le Faouët — Chapelle Ste-Barbe — Chapelle St-Fiacre — Le Faouët (10.1km/6.3mi; 2h23min; grade, equipment, access as main walk). Follow the main walk for 2h23min.

This is a beautiful walk, partly through woodland beside the river Ellé, full of contrast, and with much that is of historical and architectural interest — not least the magnificent chapels of Ste-Barbe and St-Fiacre.

Begin by walking across the square, passing to the left of the splendid 16th-century covered market. Cross the street and carry on eastwards along the Rue des Halles, opposite the market. It is signposted 'Chapelle Ste-Barbe'. In four minutes keep ahead at two crossroads. Three minutes after the second one, the tarmac ends, and the road reverts to footpath. Keep ahead, ignoring a path to the right and a track to the left, and go through the tunnel beneath the by-pass. Beyond the tunnel the track forks. However, straight ahead is a flight of stone steps. Go up these steps and keep ahead on a cobbled footpath. After 50m/yds cross a tarmac road and carry on up a delightful ancient stone-paved path, at the left of restored farm buildings. This path, the old pilgrims' way of the *pardon* of le Faouët, climbs steeply. After seven minutes, ignore a track coming up from the right; 50m/yds further on ignore a path on the left. Soon a detached belfry comes into view. Here tradition dictates that each pilgrim should ring the bell to invoke a divine benediction. Go down steps beside the belfry, to the breathtakingly-beautiful Chapelle Ste-Barbe (**30min**). The chapel was built in 1542 by Jehan de Toulbodou. Caught in a terrible storm while hunting in the forest, he had vowed to erect a chapel in honour of his patron saint in the place where he cowered, if only he would protect him.

Go down steps at the side of the chapel, and turn left to continue along the stone-paved path, heading north-west and descending quite quickly. In seven minutes ignore a path on the right and, a minute later, keep straight ahead, ignoring tracks to the right and left. Very soon you reach the end of the pilgrims' way, the sacred fountain itself. Immediately beyond the well (illustrated on page 34), you turn right and go down the right-hand side of a sloping meadow to the river Ellé (**45min**).

Turn right to follow the path beside the river, through the wood. This is possibly the loveliest part of the walk, as you can see from the photograph below. You may have noticed occasional yellow waymarks and, in seven minutes, an arrow on a tree points you off to the right, diverting you from the house ahead. (You may also notice a Petite Randonnée waymark here.) Turn right and start to re-climb the hill, turning left after 50m/yds, at a junction of tracks. A minute later, again turn left (you will see a yellow cross on the electricity pole on your right, indicating 'wrong way'). In a further two minutes, you will come to a tarmac road. Here turn right and follow the road for four minutes, to a junction with the D132 (**1h02min**).

Turn left and cross the bridge over the river Ellé. Ignore the first road on the right (to Guerlédan), immediately beyond the bridge but, in five minutes, turn right at the top of the hill, down a road signposted 'Stéroulin'. You reach this hamlet in 13 minutes. Follow the road to the right, back across the Ellé. In three minutes you come to the junction with the by-pass (**1h23min**).

Taking care, cross the main road, then turn left along the old road opposite. Follow it as it swings to the right

it is called the 'Route de Stéroulin'). Halfway up the hill here is on the left a house painted white. Immediately beyond it, turn left down a track marked with yellow blazes. Ignore the crossing track part-way down and, in six minutes, turn right on coming to a junction. Pass a farm on your left and, now on tarmac, walk to the junction with the D769 (**1h38min**). Here turn left. Just before its junction with the by-pass, turn right up a minor road to St-Fiacre. After 50m/yds leave this road, turning right along a track. You will soon be aware of white and red flashes. These are the waymarks of the GR38, which you join for a short time.

After 100m/yds go over a crossing track and, in another 100m/yds, turn left. This turning comes up just after you have passed a house and short grassy track on your right. It is very easy to miss, since the track you are on continues invitingly ahead.) Your path appears to lead into a meadow but, almost at once, you turn right to walk along a hedged-in path running almost parallel with the track you have just left. You will see both GR waymarks and a yellow arrow pointing along it.

In two minutes pass a footpath on the right which leads back to the other track, and carry on along a steadily-widening path for three minutes more, until you arrive at a glade in which there is another of Brittany's many fountains. Some 200m/yds further on, ignore a track on

the right (there is a GR 'wrong way' cross on it). A few minutes' walking brings you to a junction of tracks: turn left here, coming to a tarmac road in two minutes. Turn right on the road and, after 20m/yds, go left, to walk past farm buildings towards the 15th-century chapel of St-Fiacre (*P*14), surmounted by a fine steeple. Within is Olivier Loergan's famous rood-screen (1480), a masterpiece of late Gothic carving. There's also an attractively-sited picnic area (**2h**).

Re-trace your steps past the farm to the road. Turn right and then left, to walk back up the same track you

River Ellé

came along. This time keep straight ahead at the junction. Soon go over a crossing track, after which your own wide track narrows to a footpath. You quickly join a road (**2h08min**). Turn right and head for le Faouët. At this point you have left the GR38, although the yellow waymarks still accompany you. Bear right in six minutes, when the road forks. Ignore a road on the right two minutes later. Pass the hospital and, at **2h23min**, turn left at the T-junction to return to the square. Here look out for the menhir-like memorial to France's youngest soldier of the Great War. Corentin Carré was 15 when he enlisted.

For the second half of the walk, cross the square and head northwest along the Rue de la Croix Blanche next to the large calvary (**2h26min**). It is signposted 'Gourin' and 'Rostrenen'. After 200m, not far beyond the hotel 'Chez Lisette', turn left along the Rue de Coat en Haie, then right into the Rue de la Gare. In five minutes, having passed the Rue du Dispensaire, you rejoin the main road. Turn left, pass two streets on the left (Cours Carré and Rue du Pont Priant) and, in four minutes, turn left up a roughly-metalled road. Then turn right after 10m/yds. The road climbs for five minutes. You pass a turning on the left to the football ground; beyond here the metalling stops. In **2h53min** the way is blocked, and the track turns right for 20m/yds, then joins a road. Turn left, walking away from the water tower, and begin to descend. Ignore a track on the right. At the bottom of the hill the road becomes a gravel track into the hamlet of Cosquéric, reached in another four minutes (**3h**).

Begin to follow the road to the right, out of Cosquéric, but then turn left along a track. In two minutes turn left again, along a tarmac road which descends to wind through lightly-wooded country for nine minutes. The reason for the metalling of this section of road will become obvious, as firstly you notice the increasing amounts of litter and then the smell of smoke. It leads to le Faouët's rubbish tip. It is a curious thing, but several of these Breton walks take you past rubbish tips. Even more take you past sewage works (as you may have noticed at Stéroulin)...

Beyond the tip, the road reverts to track and, after a minute, it is blocked with vegetation. Bear right and walk at the side of the field for a minute, before regaining the original line of the track. In a further three minutes, at the

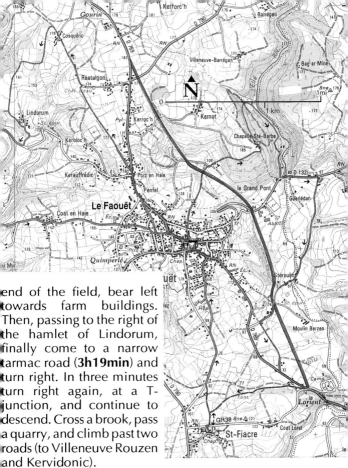

end of the field, bear left towards farm buildings. Then, passing to the right of the hamlet of Lindorum, finally come to a narrow tarmac road (**3h19min**) and turn right. In three minutes turn right again, at a T-junction, and continue to descend. Cross a brook, pass a quarry, and climb past two roads (to Villeneuve Rouzen and Kervidonic).

In **3h35min** you approach the hamlet of Keranval. Just before reaching the wayside cross, turn left for Lam-bélléguic. In four minutes ignore the road on the right to Rozenlaër and enjoy views over the Stêr Laër valley. Eight minutes later look for St Adrien's chapel, across the field on your right, and pass the hamlet of Lambélléguic. Follow the road round to the left, and then to the right, as it descends. At the bottom of the hill, ignore the track heading right to Moulin du Mur, and climb steeply up the other side of the valley (**4h**).

Having passed a road on the right, you come to Coat en Haie (**4h05min**). Follow the road back to le Faouët, entering the township in eight minutes, and arriving at a crossroads in a further 13 minutes. Go straight over, remaining on the Rue de Coat en Haie as far as the junction with the D790 (**4h32min**). Turn right and, in three minutes, you arrive back at the market square (**4h35min**).

16 BESIDE THE RIVER BLAVET

See photograph page 17

Distance: 19km/11.8mi; 4h   **Grade:** easy

Equipment: walking boots if wet, otherwise comfortable shoes or trainers, sunhat, suncream, raingear, picnic, water

How to get there and return: 🚌 to Pontivy. Although passenger trains no longer run to Pontivy, it is connected by bus to Rennes, Vannes, Auray, Lorient and Loudéac. The bus station (*gare routière*) is adjacent to the old railway station. 🚗: to Pontivy in north Morbihan. Park beside the river, or at the Place A Briand, between the river and the Rue Nationale. Walk to the river and turn right.

Short walk: Pontivy — Guernal Lock — Stival — Pontivy (11.2km/7mi; 2h20min; grade, equipment, access as above). Follow the main wall for 1h. Cross the canal here, by the iron footbridge above the dam, then turn right along the D156. Follow it as it bends to left and right for 500m/yds (6min). Then, as it bends sharply to the right once more, you will see a tarmac road on the left leading to a farm. In the angle of the two roads there is a farm track. Turn left up this track and, at the top of the field, turn left. Now pick up the main walk at the 2h50min-point.

During the Napoleonic Wars, French ports were blockaded by the British Royal Navy. Napoleon's remedy was to link up the rivers of Brittany and create a great canal the length of the province, to connect Brest with Nantes. Today some of the prettiest walking in Brittany can be found along its towpath, as can be seen in the photograph on page 17.

Leave the bus station and **start out** by walking westwards, across the Place A Brard and down the Rue Gambetta. Turn right along the Rue Nationale. Should you wish to begin the day by exploring Pontivy, 500m/yds will bring you to the centre of the old town, and another 350m/yds to the Duke de Rohan's castle. Otherwise, take the first turning on the left by St Joseph's Church and walk to the river. Turn right along the Quai d'Arcole and pass under a bridge. To your right is the Place A Briand (*possible starting point for motorists*). Continue through the other parking area mentioned above, until you come to the second (and main) bridge over the Blavet. The Old Town is to your right now.

Cross the bridge and immediately turn right, following the sign 'Centre Hospitalier' (**12min**). Bear left beyond the hospital, then turn right along the Rue des Trois Frères Cornec, beside an arm of the river. In five minutes turn right, signposted 'Station des Eaux'. After passing the waterworks, cross the canal via an iron footbridge, then follow a tarmac path beside the canal — to a second bridge, which you also cross.

Turn left now, and walk along the tarmac towpath, with

a sports ground on your right (**20min**). The path is pleasantly shaded and peaceful, much frequented by wagtails and jays and little else. Look out for the old kilometre stones. The distances are shown on the sides. You will pass the first of three locks after 13 minutes. Pass the village of Stival on the far side of the river (**50min**) and, soon, a road on the right.

At **1h** you reach the second lock, the Ecluse de Guernal. *If you are doing the Short walk, cross the canal here.*) Beyond the lock the tarred surface of the towpath ends, as does the shade from the trees. You have reached the halfway-point of your walk alongside the canal. In 13 minutes ignore a footpath on your right which leads over a wooden footbridge to the hamlet of le Grével. The hamlet ahead and to the left is Locqueltas. Look for its chapel. At about **1h30min** you should be able to see the belfry of the chapel at Carmez to the right; soon afterwards, the dam and third lock (Porzo) come into view. This is where you cross the canal, at first by the bridge on the lock gate, and then by the iron bridge over the dam. Once across the river, walk between a stream and a house, towards a track. The track takes you between tall trees, and you join a tarmac road, where you turn left (**1h40min**).

There is fairly open country now, save for a wooded knoll on your right. In eight minutes cross over the D156 and continue to climb gently. The views as you rise are quite extensive. You pass three roads on the right, two of them to Guernalo and, at **2h07min**, you come to the grounds of the Château de Beauregard, discernible through the trees. The road bends sharply left by the gate (which also leads to a nursing home). In a further eight minutes, when you are facing a calvary, turn left at the junction with the D15. Go downhill for three minutes, but keep straight ahead at the fork at the bottom, where the main road swings right. Look at the back of the road sign, and you will see the white and red flashes which mark the route of Grande Randonnée footpaths. This one is the GR37, which we join for the remainder of the walk.

Soon bear left at the next fork, along the R35 to Fournan. Three minutes later, follow the road round to the right, ignoring both tracks to the left. Bear right when you reach the buildings of Fournan (**2h24min**), then turn left at the -junction. Continue along a tarmac road, with attractive views to both sides. In seven minutes pass a road on your right. To your left you can see the chapels of Carmez and, beyond, Neulliac. In four minutes go over a crossing track

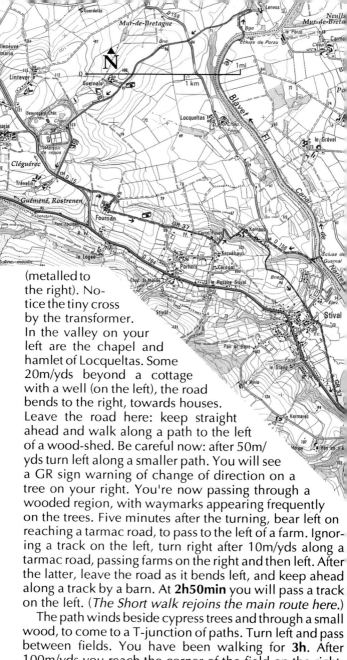

(metalled to
the right). No-
tice the tiny cross
by the transformer.
In the valley on your
left are the chapel and
hamlet of Locqueltas. Some
20m/yds beyond a cottage
with a well (on the left), the road
bends to the right, towards houses.
Leave the road here: keep straight
ahead and walk along a path to the left
of a wood-shed. Be careful now: after 50m/
yds turn left along a smaller path. You will see
a GR sign warning of change of direction on a
tree on your right. You're now passing through a
wooded region, with waymarks appearing frequently
on the trees. Five minutes after the turning, bear left on
reaching a tarmac road, to pass to the left of a farm. Ignoring a track on the left, turn right after 10m/yds along a
tarmac road, passing farms on the right and then left. After
the latter, leave the road as it bends left, and keep ahead
along a track by a barn. At **2h50min** you will pass a track
on the left. (*The Short walk rejoins the main route here.*)

The path winds beside cypress trees and through a small
wood, to come to a T-junction of paths. Turn left and pass
between fields. You have been walking for **3h**. After
100m/yds you reach the corner of the field on the right.
Walk ahead for 20m/yds, to the left of the hedge, and
enter another field. Stay by the hedge and, in 10m/yds,
turn right and cross the end of a sunken, overgrown track.

Turn left on the far side and walk down the field, keeping to the right of the hedge. Pass to the right of a shed. There are allotments on your right now. In the far left-hand corner of the field, bear left on a path which runs beside the sunken track, before finally joining it.

At **3h12min** you reach the village of Stival. Ignore the road on your left; keep ahead. After 20m/yds pass a road on the right and, in another 20m/yds, keep ahead at the junction with the D156. A minute later ignore a road on the right, then one on the left. Now the D156 bends to the right. Unless you wish to follow it to the 15th-century church of St Meriadoc, with stained glass windows by Jehan Le Flamant (1552), leave it now: bear left past the school, ignore a track on the right by the school grounds, and turn right when the road forks (**3h18min**). Follow this straight lane for ten minutes, when it will turn left and run parallel to the D764. Walk between the road and the river, then fork left along a wide metalled footpath. In three minutes turn left at the T-junction (signposted 'Piscine de Plein Air'), and ignore the two roads opposite. In two minutes bear left when the road forks again; pass a picnic area, beyond which you turn left over a concrete footbridge, towards the swimming pool. Turn right, pass to the back of the pool and walk back into Pontivy beside a narrow arm of the river . In **3h46min** the GR37 turns left towards the water-works where you began your walk, but now you must keep ahead and continue beside the river for another two minutes. Beyond the hospital, you come to a T-junction: turn left, away from the river, and follow the road round to the big bridge over the Blavet.

Beyond the bridge, turn right and walk beside the canal to the car parks. To continue to the bus station, go under a bridge, turn left up the Rue Linéville, cross over the Rue Marengo, pass St Joseph's Church, and turn right along the Rue Nationale. Take the first turning on the left, go up the Rue Gambetta, and cross the square to return to the *gare routière* (**4h**).

17 LE VAL SANS RETOUR

See map page 114

Distance: 12km/7.5mi; 2h54min   **Grade:** moderate

Equipment: walking boots preferably, especially if wet, otherwise comfortable shoes or trainers, sunhat, suncream, raingear, picnic, water

How to get there and return: 🚌 to Tréhorenteuc. Leave the D766 (Ploërmel to Dinan road) 10km north of Ploërmel, heading for Néant-sur-Yvel. Then take the D154 to Tréhorenteuc. Bear right through the village (following the sign for Ploërmel on the D141). You pass a lovely old manor house; there is a visitors' car park just beyond it.

This is a walk through the magical forest of Brocéliande wherein lives the wizard Merlin, eternally enchanted by his beloved, the fairy Viviane. For it was in Brittany that the mediaeval French poets located the Arthurian cycle of legends, above all here in Paimpont Forest.

Standing with your back to the village, **begin the walk** along the wide track on your left (*P*19), heading southeast (signposted 'Le Val sans Retour'). As far as the hamlet of Beauvais, the walk follows the route of the GR37, so look for the white and red flashes which will help you to identify your way. In six minutes the track turns left and climbs steeply. Three minutes later, follow it to the right, past a wooden barrier. In a further two minutes, turn right down a well-signposted path, into the wood. (At least, it used to be a wood, and no doubt will one day be a wood again. A forest fire in 1990 left this bit of Brocéliande looking very charred and sorry for itself.) But ponder well before you set off: this path leads to the Valley of No Return, that Vale of False Lovers where Viviane's rival, Morgane le Fay, tempts the unwary, and whence no knight unfaithful to his lady has ever emerged.

In one minute turn right (but, before doing so, enjoy the view from the rock ahead). A minute later, go right again, by a large rock on which there is a GR waymark. You descend through what remains of the burned trees, until you see a pool below you. This is the 'Fairies' Mirror' where the forest folk come to comb their locks. Follow the path to the right, over a footbridge, and walk round the pool; then turn left at a T-junction (**20min**), to continue beside it. Soon bear right along a narrow footpath, with a stream on your left. Two minutes later, use the waymarked path on the right, when the path forks, still keeping to the right of the stream. In four minutes you cross a brook and, two minutes later, use the stepping stones along the edge of the stream — or clamber up the rocks on your right, to arrive at the same place (**30min**). Continue along the path and, eventually, cross the

tream by stepping stones, as you approach the dam. The
GR takes you by a roundabout way now: turn left to cross
the dam and climb steps up the cliff. Turn right, and walk
high above the lake. This extra bit of effort enables you
to take advantage of the fine view of the lake from above
(photograph page 112). When the path forks, turn right
and go down to lake level again, then cross a footbridge
and turn left, to regain your original path (**41min**).

Still beside the stream, make your way through the trees
for two minutes, at which time you will come to GR
signposts and a map. Keep straight ahead on the GR37,
signposted 'Vallée de l'Aff'. In four minutes you reach a
wooden barrier and turn right at a junction of tracks, where
you begin to climb out of the valley. Six minutes later
ignore a track on the left and, three minutes further on,
leave the woodland on a wide track. In four minutes turn
left at the junction with a tarmac road. You have now
been walking for **1h**. After five minutes turn right at a T-
junction by a well, in the hamlet of La Guette. Pass a road
on the right in four minutes, then Beauvais farm and, in
1h14min, the chapel and holy well of St Anthony
bordering a road to the right (which you ignore). Two
minutes after this you come to a crossroads, presided over
by a wooden cross, by the well of St Roch.

Turn left here, leaving the GR37, which goes on ahead.
Fork left for Doucette in four minutes and, after 250m/yds,
follow the road round to the right (just after passing a farm
drive on the left). A minute later fork left on a wide track
leading into the forest, ignoring the path to the right
100m/yds along. Two minutes later you come to a crossroads. Turn right and walk towards a telecommunications
tower. On reaching it (**1h36min**), bear left to pass it, then
turn left. On your right is an old wood, while to your left
are newly-planted commercial conifers.

Head due north now, between the trees, walking
through an open grassy space for some 500m/0.3mi. In
seven minutes you meet a track coming from the left,
which bends north here. Keep straight ahead and, in
50m/yds, go over a crossing track, to continue northwest
through old woodland. In six minutes you reach a tarmac
road, on a bend. Turn left and, in five minutes, turn left
again at the first crossroads, in the direction of Néant-sur-
Ével and Tréhorenteuc.

In four minutes you pass a forest track on the left (**2h**),
followed by two on the right. The road goes downhill and,
at the bottom of the dip (**2h06min**), there is a wide opening

The lake at Le Val sans Retour

to a second track on the left. Turn down this track. Notice the result of coppicing on this ancient deciduous woodland. Nearly all the trees have multiple trunks that sprang from the stumps of previously-felled trees. In four minutes the track swings to the right and begins to go downhill. Five minutes later keep ahead over a crossing track. Your track winds for four minutes, before the next crossing track is reached (beyond one or two rock outcrops that offer almost the only suitable places to stop and picnic en route). Keep straight ahead through a logging area. Soon you pass track number 49 (on the right; **2h21min**) and two minutes later, number 47. You may glimpse a quarry through the trees, the source of the red shale which surfaces so many of the tracks in this region.

At **2h30min** you are walking parallel with, and above, the Val sans Retour to your left. Ignore a footpath on your left leading down to it and, three minutes later, a track going off the same way. In six minutes pass more rock outcrops. At **2h44min** you come to a GR37 signpost. Take the path to the left and, beyond the outcrop, go over a crossing path for a superb view down into the valley and the lake you passed earlier. Then return towards the outcrop and turn left along the crossing path (ie, continue in the same direction as you were heading on the wide track). This path is marked with yellow circles; it takes you along the edge of the cliff for five minutes, until you turn right at the next rock outcrop, to retrace your steps along the path by which you first entered the vale. Turn left on reaching your outgoing track and, in two minutes, turn left at the barrier, to return to the car park (**2h54min**).

8 FOREST OF PAIMPONT

See photograph page 18
Distance: 13.8km/8.6mi; 3h10min

Grade: moderate

Equipment: walking boots preferably, certainly if wet, otherwise comfortable shoes or trainers, sunhat, suncream, raingear, picnic, water

How to get there and return: Only accessible by 🚗: Leave the N24 (Ploërmel to Rennes road) 8km east of Ploërmel, just beyond Campénéac. Take the D312 for Paimpont. This becomes the D40. After 6.6km you come to a crossroads, with two roads on the left, the second one signposted 'Tréhorenteuc' and 'Le Pertuis Neanti'. On the right there is a 'No Through Road'. Park here in Le Châtenay (beside the bus shelter if there is room, or drive a further 200m/yds along the D40 and park on the left). After your walk I recommend you follow the D40 into the village of Paimpont (6km *P*18), to see its lake and old abbey.

This walk is similar to nearby Walk 17 in the Val sans Retour; it offers the slightly claustrophobic experience of walking for an hour and a half along a narrow winding path through unbroken woodland. It is best undertaken in company. Be assured, however, that it is quite impossible to get lost! The remainder of the walk is also through ancient forest, but on wide straight tracks.

To begin the walk, turn your back on the D40 and walk down the 'No Through Road'. The white and red bands of the GR37 will help guide you for the next hour and a half. After passing between cottages, the tarmac gives way to red shale and enters the forest. On your right a GR waymark warns of a change of direction: in 20m/yds turn left. This footpath takes you down to the river Aff, beside which you will walk for the next 6km/3.7mi. Ignore a footpath on the right a minute along and, seven minutes later, cross a brook (the Ruisseau de St-Jean) via stepping-stones. In two minutes keep ahead, ignoring a path to the right, and go over another brook. At **21min** pass (but do not cross) a footbridge on the left and, in the course of the next ten minutes, cross two more brooks flowing into the Aff. The white and red waymarks appear every 200m/yds or so.

At **41min** take care where the river bank has collapsed. After **55min** a more open area of moss-covered rocks provides an idyllic picnic setting (photograph page 18). At **1h06min** the river flows round boulders in what is known in Brittany as a 'chaos', of which the most famous is at Huelgoat (Walk 4). After about **1h20min** you may hear the sound of gunfire; you are now level with the firing range of the St-Cyr Military Academy, 1km to your right. At **1h27min** a sunken path suddenly appears to the left: your path crosses it, runs parallel with it for a few metres/yards, and then recrosses it. Stay on what is now

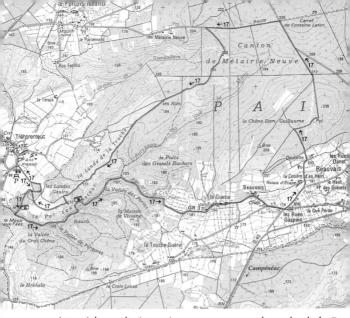

a quite wide path, ignoring a narrow path to the left. Pas
a number of curious stone markers beside the pa
(**1h30min**), and ignore a second path on the left. Soo
you will see a tarred road ahead, which you reach besid
a wooden *crêperie*. Follow it to its junction with the D7
(**1h33min**), where you turn left. You leave the GR3
which continues to follow the river Aff. In three minute
the road bends left, but your way is straight ahead, up
forest track. In two minutes, ignore a track on the righ
cross the road and continue up the path opposite*, throug
trees. When you re-emerge on the road continue walkin
northeast for 300m/yds.

At **1h43min**, the D71 turns half left, and a forest trac
continues straight ahead. Ignore both of them: your wa
now lies along the red-surfaced gravel track to your lef
beyond a barrier. This is the Ligne de Roche Plate, an
you are going to follow it (with only one change c
direction) for 42 minutes, passing many other tracks o
the left and right. Notice that the trees at the start of thes
paths have numbers painted on them. These enable yo
to pinpoint your location in relation to the walking note
at **1h52min** for example, the path on the right is numbere
24 and 21, while the next track is 20. At **1h57min** th
track dips to cross a little valley, with a small pool at th
bottom. Some 50m/yds beyond the pool, the track fork.
Keep straight ahead. In **2h** pass in front of the dwellin

*Should this footpath become impenetrably overgrown, ignore it, an
follow the road up to the right instead.

nown as Roche Plate and go down the footpath opposite. oon you go over an S-shaped crossing track and, at **h04min**, you meet it again. Ignore the track to the left.

At **2h13min** there is a track on the left (tree no 19). In ree minutes your track turns right, heading northwest. On the right here is path 18. After 250m/yds there is a ath to the left (tree no 16), and you descend to cross

other little valley and brook. At **2h22min** there is other track on the left, also with a tree numbered 16! owever, keep straight ahead for three minutes, until you ome to a little clearing and a crossing track (**2h25min**). ere you turn left (southwest) along a broad track, the gne de L'Orgeril, by tree no 14. (If you miss this turning, under 1km/0.5mi you would come to the D40, where eft turn would bring you back to your car in 2km/1.2mi.)

Descend to another little clearing and pool in three inutes. Soon pass an overgrown track on the right, then o more (at three-minute intervals). Two minutes after e third track, your track divides. Ignore the first track on e left but, after 10m/yds, fork left (**2h38min**). Follow the ath, now somewhat overgrown, as it circles to the right und the gardens and cottages of L'Orgeril, to a junction ith a tarmac road: turn left. After 12 minutes pass two ads on the right. Four minutes later pass a road on the ft, before reaching the D40, where you turn left (**3h**). At e top of the hill your car awaits you (**3h10min**).

19 DINAN

See also photograph page 21

Distance: 16.2km/10mi; 5h13min   **Grade:** fairly strenuou

Equipment: walking boots preferably, certainly if wet, otherwise con
fortable shoes or trainers, long trousers (for protection from nettle
sunhat, suncream, raingear, picnic, water

How to get there and return: 🚂 to Dinan from Rennes or St-Malo
Change at Dol. 🚌 to Dinan from Rennes or Dinard. 🚗: Dinan, in Côte
d'Armor, is best approached from the east, via the river Rance, on th
N176 (not for ease or convenience, but for the magnificence of i
impact). Park in the town centre or by the railway station.

Short walk: Dinan — Léhon — Dinan (7.1km/4.4mi; 1h40min; grad
easy; equipment: comfortable shoes, sunhat, raingear; access as ma
walk). Follow the main walk as far as the Gothic bridge over the rive
Rance, then pick up the main walk at the 3h50min-point.

This walk divides into two parts, one long, the othe
short, beside the river Rance. Both begin at the Gothi
bridge. The Short walk can be undertaken by anyone an
follows the Rance to the picturesque historic village c
Léhon, returning by the old road. The longer walk is fc
the young, at least at heart. It goes out along an excitin
path created and maintained by the staff of the Dina
auberge de jeunesse (youth hostel). At times it may requi
care and a certain agility, as it climbs and twists amon
the woods and cliffs bordering the river. Then, where rive
and estuary meet, you cross the dam and return to Dina
along the towpath.

For the benefit of those arriving by train or bus, **th
walk begins** at the railway station, which is adjacent t
the bus station. Others may prefer to make their own wa
to the Gothic bridge across the river Rance.

Walk diagonally left, away from the station, along th
Rue Carnot. Cross over the Place Général Leclerc at th
end and, bearing slightly left, walk between the rampar
of mediaeval Dinan and the car park. Pass to the right c
the war memorial and continue across a large open spac
dedicated to *pétanque* (bowls). Climb up steps at the fa
end, skirt the car park to the right and, in two minute
go up more steps on your left. Walk now beneath plan
trees, with the Rue Leconte de Lisle below on the left an
the town walls still on your right. In three minutes pas
the St-Malo gate on your right and continue straight aheac
down Le Roquet. Turn left at the T-junction (to your rig
is the Jerzual Gate, shown on page 21) and continue t
descend steeply down the attractive Rue du Petit Fort, t
arrive at the river Rance (**15min**). (*If you are doing th
Short walk, now turn to page 120 and pick up the wa
from the 3h50min-point.*)

Car tour 7; Picnic 22: The port of Dinan. You can just see the Gothic bridge on the left.

Cross the river by the so-called 'Gothic bridge', the little mediaeval bridge in front of you, and immediately turn left. As you follow the river northwards, you will notice the yellow bands used to waymark this walk. In 14 minutes pass to the left of the sewage works and continue ahead, no longer on tarmac. Beyond the sewage works the track divides into three paths. Choose the middle one, which crosses open ground and enters a wood; here you will see a PR (Petite Randonnée) waymark, on your left. The path, cut through an earthen bank, bears right. Keep left, to the entrance to a field on your right. At this point the footpath is quite wide but, a minute later (**34min**), it narrows considerably and passes through a wild, damp region of nettles. This is the old river ('Marais' on the map). Before the canal straightened it out in 1832, the Rance flowed in an awkward loop where you are now walking. There is still a brook here, which you cross — first on an old footbridge and then on a dead tree trunk (the first test of your agility). After following the path to the right, you face the second agility test, as you scramble up steep earthen steps and over a fallen tree. Beyond the tree, bear right and climb the slope to a wall opposite. Follow the path to the left and, in a minute, emerge on a tarmac road by the Château de Grillemont (**46min**; photograph page 121). Here a signpost indicates Lyvet, 5km distant. Turn left and, in four minutes, pass on your right the Château de Landeboulou; then turn left at a T-junction.

Ignore a path on the right after 50m/yds (at the end of a wall), but turn right in a further 50m/yds, along a second, well waymarked path, at the point where the road itself

117

bends left. This path, initially quite wide, leads you dow
through trees towards the river, reached in five minut
(**1h**). The path now runs beside the river. It is mostly
good condition, although occasionally it shows signs
erosion and demands care. At **1h06min** you reach anoth
valley. This is Port Josselin, as before an area of nettl
and luxuriant growth, where in ancient times the riv
was fordable. Again cross a tributary by a footbridge, the
follow the path as it twists and winds away from the rive
In three minutes go up steps and begin another stee
climb. As you near the top, the path forks. Bear le
following the waymarks upwards and, in two minute
you will be at the top of the cliff and walking parallel
the river, with an arable field on your right (**1h15min**).

The path is quite narrow, with a steep drop down t
water meadows on the left. There are fine views over th
river, which widens enormously ahead. Opposite lie
Taden, built on the site of a Gallo-Roman village which
once stood beside the ford. Carry on following the
waymarked path high above the river for nine
minutes, until a rock outcrop on the left
affords magnificent views. This is the Saut
à la Puce ('Flea's Leap'). The path
begins to descend increasingly
steeply and, in five minutes,
joins a tarmac road: turn left
here and, then, almost
at once, bear right

y a signpost labelled 'Chantoiseau'). A bridge takes you ver the Ruisseau Ste-Geneviève, then you pass a house n your left. Beyond the house, turn left along a track (a ellow 'X' on a telegraph pole warns you against continuing along the road). This brings you to the river once ore. The track ends at the river. Turn right and follow a arrow path and then steep steps. Climb for two minutes, to a junction of tracks. Turn left, soon to struggle briefly with brambles. In eight minutes the path bends right and descends quickly to the muddy Val Orieux. Cross the brook via an ingeniously-designed stile and stepping stones, then turn left. Pass under two fallen trees and regain the river. The path now runs beside the river, but climbs into light woodland.

At **1h46min** the path forks. Turn left, pass a wooden barrier, and soon regain the top of the cliff, again with arable fields to your right. At **1h50min** a signpost informs you that the projecting spur on your left is the 'Eperon Barré', where once an Iron Age fort dominated the river. Ignore a short track to the left and continue along a wide track: in two minutes it turns right. Two minutes later it heads eft, towards the hamlet of Le Châtelier. On reaching the e Châtelier' sign, your way is ultimately straight ahead, ut first make a short detour. Turn left (on tarmac) and en go right, when you come to a path. After 10m/yds ou enjoy a lovely view over the river and the marina at yvet's port. Retrace your steps along the path to the road, en turn left. When you come to the sign, turn left to ontinue in your original direction. Walking through the amlet (**2h**), ignore a road on the right and, after 50m/yds, rn left, down a narrow tarmac lane. Then bear right along narrow cobbled path. In a minute go under a fallen tree; gnore a path to the left beyond it. The cobbles give out ow, and the path is more than a little overgrown with ettles and brambles for a short time, as you cross one ore valley, with stepping stones over a brook.

Once you have climbed out of that valley, the path runs eside a field for 60m/yds and brings you to a road

(**2h09min**). Here another signpost tells you it is only 1k
to Lyvet. Turn left. In three minutes there is another *poin*
de vue on the left. Opposite is le Petit Lyvet. In four minute
you are within 50m/yds of the junction with the main road
the D57. On your left is a sunken path; turn down it. I
four minutes the path joins a tarmac road. To your rig
are a cross and grotto, but turn left and go down to th
river, joining it at the port of Lyvet.

Turn right and walk beside the river as far as the da
ahead, then turn left and cross the river along the dam
not the viaduct. To your left is the river, to your right th
tidal estuary. Finish crossing by going over the loc
footbridge (**2h30min**). Turn left past the lock-keeper
cabin and follow the towpath back to Dinan. In 12 minute
you pass the port of le Petit Lyvet that you saw from L
Châtelier and, a quarter of an hour later, a well-equippe
picnic area (**3h**). This is the setting for *P*22 (an hour's wa
from Dinan via the towpath). Many gulls and ducks fre
quent the Rance, but look too for cormorants. A furthe
15 minutes brings you to L'Asile des Pêcheurs, on the si
of the ancient ford; a road on the right leads to Taden.

At about **3h30min** you will be opposite the valley
the old river, above which stands the Château de Grille
mont. The sewage works are located where the rive
formerly looped back, and you can see where the ne
river was created by cutting the canal. By **3h50min** yo
are back at the Gothic bridge. (*Pick up the notes belo*
if you are doing the Short walk.)

To continue the walk, cross the river once more. Imme
diately turn right, along the narrow D2, and walk besid
the river, past the rowing club and under the viadu
(1852). This part of the walk has long been the favouri
Sunday afternoon stroll of the Dinannais. After 20 minute
you pass an islet in the river and a lock (**4h10min**). Seve
minutes later, turn right to cross the river by another o
bridge, then bear right. This is the village of Léhon. O
the right is the Abbaye de St-Magloire, founded in 85(
with a 14th-century refectory and 17th-century cloister
The church contains the tombs of the Beaumanoir family
including that of Jehan de Beaumanoir, hero of the Comba
des Trente (1351; see page 37).

Having passed through the village with its 17th- an
18th-century houses, at once turn left and follow the roa
signposted 'école', up to the ruins of a 13th-century cast
(turn right at the top of the hill, up a steep gradient). Afte
visiting the castle, do not return down the road, but be

The Château de Grillemont and the river Rance (Picnic 22)

right at the junction, and descend a path to the D12 (**4h36min**). Turn right, and walk beneath the ramparts and towers, which look much more imposing from down here.

Keep straight ahead at the crossroads, in the direction of Dinan, but turn down the next road on the right, the Rue du Moulin au Duc. After 75m/yds take the first turning on the left, the tiny Rue Beaumanoir, and climb up steps. At the top, ignore a road bending sharply backwards, and follow this elegant street for ten minutes into Dinan. At the end of the Rue Beaumanoir, bear right across the Place St-Louis and enter the Old Town through the St-Louis Gate. Crossing the Rue Général de Gaulle, continue in the same (northerly) direction along the Rue de Léhon and on into the Rue de l'Horloge. On your right is the tourist information office (**5h**). Continuing in the same direction, walk first along the Rue de la Poissonerie and then the Rue de l'Ecole. Leave the Old Town through the St-Malo Gate, turn left, and follow the promenade above the Rue de Leconte de Lisle, to the Place du Général Leclerc. Then take the Rue Carnot to the station (**5h13min**).

20 BON-REPOS ABBEY AND QUENECAN FOREST

See also photograph page 24

Distance: 17.6km/11mi; 4h15min   **Grade:** moderate

Equipment: walking boots if wet, otherwise comfortable shoes or trainers, sunhat, suncream, raingear, picnic, water

How to get there and return: 🚌: The Carhaix/Loudéac service stops at Bon-Repos, between Gouarec and Mur-de-Bretagne. Walk southward from the bus stop down the D15a, which joins the main road just before it crosses the river Daoulas. 🚗: From Mur-de-Bretagne in southern Côtes d'Armor, drive east along the N164 for 16km. Turn left down the D15 just before crossing the Daoulas. There is a car park on the right.

Shorter walks

1 Bon-Repos — Quénécan Forest — Bon-Repos (11.5km/7.2mi; 3h; grade, equipment, access as above). Follow the main walk for 3h.

2 Bon-Repos — Gorges du Daoulas — Bon-Repos (6km/3.8m; 1h15min; grade, equipment, access as above). Pick up the main walk at the 3h-point and follow it to the end.

NB: Few of the forest tracks in the text are shown on the IGN map.

T he Cistercian abbey of Bon-Repos ('Good Sleep') was founded in 1184 by Alain, Vicomte de Rohan, a chronic insomniac, in gratitude for the good night's sleep that he finally enjoyed after hunting in the Forest of Quénécan. It was rebuilt in the 14th century, although most of what remains is the work of the early 18th century. The abbey was destroyed during the Revolution. The ruin (**P**15) will no doubt have first call on your attention, but thereafter the walk takes you through the ancient forest, still home to deer and boar, and beside the Nantes-Brest Canal. Passing the abbey once more, you continue to the remarkable gallery graves or *allées couvertes* of Liscuis, and you complete the walk by descending through the Gorges du Daoulas.

From the parking area turn right along the D15a and **start the walk** by crossing the river Blavet, leaving the abbey to your left. Once across the bridge, turn right and follow the little hedged-in footpath between houses. This is *not* the asphalt path beside the river. You may notice white and red bands on a tree beside the path, and an arrow pointing to it. Much of the first half of the walk follows the GR37, and you will have the assistance of these waymarks for the next two and a half hours.

In **5min** the path forks: bear left uphill. Two minutes later, there is another junction. Bear right this time, then follow the path through the wood for nine minutes, before coming to the next junction of paths. Again keep to the right. (You will see that the path to the left bears a white and red cross indicating 'wrong way'.) In nine minutes

(25min into the walk) look out for the waymark on your left. This has double bands with an arrow bending left. Such marking warns that you are about to leave the path you are on, to change direction. Leave your wide path at this junction, and bear left. The flashes on the first tree on the left along your new path confirm that you are now on the correct route. You will continue to meet waymarks at about two-minute intervals. So far you have been more or less following the 140 metres contour (ie, walking at about 460 feet). Now you begin to climb to a height of some 260m/850ft.

At **30min** take no notice of a path to the left. Two minutes later keep ahead, when you cross a track. Three minutes after that, again ignore a track to the left. Now you'll see the pretty farmhouse of Le Léty behind the trees on your right. Bear right, to pass to the left of this farm. (Take no notice of any waymarks directing you into the wood at this point, since the woodland route is by no means clear, being quite overgrown.) In two minutes turn left, at the junction with a tarmac road leading to Le Léty.

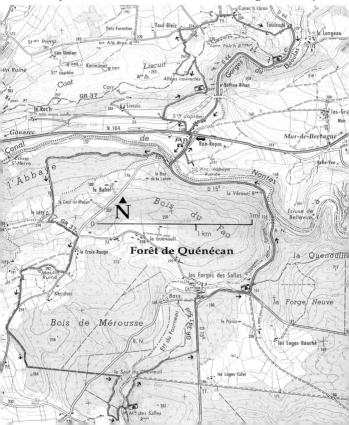

At **46min** you arrive at a crossroads. Turn right and climb past a road on your left and the Croix-Rouge farm. At the brow of the hill (**50min**) look for the GR 'change of direction' sign on a telegraph pole and, just as you pass a farm drive on the left, turn right along a track which leads to a footpath. The directions may seem a little confusing for the next ten minutes, but do not worry: the route is clearly waymarked with white and red bands.

In two minutes the path takes you through a clump of trees and past a concrete pylon bearing a waymark. A similarly-marked pine tree is encountered, then you go on between gorse bushes, finally curving round to a ruined windmill. Beyond the windmill, continue on a slightly wider track. In two minutes keep straight ahead, when you meet a crossing track. In a further two minutes (**1h**), ignore the track forking back to your right. A minute later, turn left along a narrow roughly-tarred road and, after 20m/yds, turn left again, at the next junction. Follow the track towards a house, ignoring tracks to right and left. Carry on past the house, heading due south along what is again a roughly-tarred road.

At **1h06min** turn right at a T-junction. In four minutes follow the waymarks to the left and re-enter the wood along a narrow forest track. At **1h15min** bear right at a fork, along the better track, which soon bends left. In two minutes the track turns sharply to the left. It is very wide now and heads almost due east. In five minutes keep ahead at the crossing track, and do the same two minutes later. Stay on this wide track until, in **1h30min**, you come to a tarmac road.

Cross the road and continue along a forest track. In two minutes pass a path on the left. You have now reached another tricky section but, again, it is well waymarked. In two minutes the path turns right (ie, southwards) and takes you past a rock outcrop on your left, overlooking a steepish little gorge. This is the Saut du Chevreuil ('Roe-Deer's Leap'). Follow the path as it forks right (southwest) here, twisting between trees, but clearly visible. At **1h37min** the path forks again: bear left round a fallen tree. In four minutes the path goes through a wall. A minute later notice the 'change of direction' sign and turn left. There is a house over to your right, and an earthen bank beside the path. In two minutes fork left down a sunken path, which continues to bend to the left; you find yourself heading back in a northerly direction. After three minutes the path turns right and crosses a stream in one of the most picturesque settings so far encountered on the walk. Beyond the stream there is a GR signpost. Your way is left along the GR341, northwards beside the brook. In eight minutes you will see above you on the left the Saut du Chevreuil, as you cross a track. (This track is the eastward continuation of the one you were following earlier, which was interrupted by the gorge.) Not only do you stand a good chance of seeing deer in these woods, but shy wild boar too.

You have now been walking for **2h**. Ignore a footbridge on your left and, soon, you will see a lake (the Etang du Fourneau) between the trees. In four minutes cross over a footpath then, a minute later, make your way round a fallen tree. Follow the now quite narrow footpath to its junction with the D15a, where you turn left. After eight minutes this straight road bends right, but keep ahead on a track here, for a view of the château and hamlet of Les Forges des Salles. Until the beginning of the 19th century there were several iron furnaces working here. Bear right at the T-junction in front of the château, then go left along the D15a, when the track rejoins the road. Follow the road round the lake. At **2h25min** bear left at the road junction. Very soon now the GR341 leaves you; it goes away to the right, while you follow the road northwards beside the stream.

You cross the stream in **2h36min**, just where it flows into the Nantes-Brest Canal. Stay on the road, pass in front of the magnificent ruins of Bon-Repos (shown below), then recross the canal and return to the car park (**3h**).

For the second part of the walk you continue north, forking left through the car park and picnic area, beside the Daoulas, another tributary stream of the canalised river Blavet. In three minutes turn left along the N164, cross the Daoulas bridge, and pass the D44 on your right. Beyond it is a house

The ruins of Bon-Repos Abbey, seen through the trees beside the Nantes-Brest Canal; see also photograph page 24.

and, just beyond the house, another road. Turn right here (signposted 'Allées Couvertes du Liscuis'). You are back on the GR341, so watch for the waymarks. The road swings left and right, passing a track to the right. In two minutes turn right along a well-marked track, which climbs to give you excellent views, first over the abbey and then over the Gorges du Daoulas. You pass an old slate quarry and the remains of the slate workers (*ardoisiers'*) hut. At **3h21min** turn left on reaching a crossing path and, three minutes later, you will come to the first of the *allées couvertes*, or elongated dolmens.

These tombs are neolithic, between four and six thousand years old, and were originally covered with earth or stones. Follow the path to the second dolmen, then turn right and continue to the third, some 120m/yds further on. From there carry on along the path to the right, beyond the dolmen, until you rejoin the continuation of your original track (**3h31min**). Turn left, and follow the path down the side of a field. As it swings right out of the field, immediately turn left down a crossing hedged-in path. (This path should be clear. If, however, it has been allowed to overgrow, keep straight ahead on the road through the hamlet.) At the end of the path, turn right along a narrow road, passing a wayside cross. In two minutes pass a road on the right (which you will come down if you walk through the hamlet) and another on the left. Soon the road bends left and then right, with a track on the left.

After 20m/yds the GR341 forks left at a Y-junction, and you bid it farewell here: keep ahead on a poorly-surfaced road and, in two minutes, turn right at a T-junction. The road climbs, passes a narrow road on the right and joins the D44 (**3h48min**). Turn right to walk down through the scenic Gorges du Daoulas for 25 minutes.

You arrive once more at the junction with the N164. This time turn left and, after crossing the bridge, turn right, to retrace your steps beside the Daoulas — back to the car park or the bus stop (**4h15min**).

21 THE PINK GRANITE COAST

See also photograph page 19

Distance: 22.5km/14mi; 4h50min   **Grade:** easy

Equipment: comfortable shoes or trainers (but if it is wet, boots would be an asset for the Vallée des Traouiéros section), sunhat, suncream, raingear, picnic, water, swimwear, towel

How to get there and return: 🚐 to Trégastel-Plage on the north coast of Côtes-d'Armor. Take the D65 northwest from Lannion to Trébeurden, then follow the beautiful Breton Corniche to Trégastel-Plage. On reaching Trégastel-Plage, when you come to the Hôtel de la Corniche, turn left towards 'La Grève Blanche' and park in the large car park on the right.

Shorter walks: see page 129.

This walk in Côtes-d'Armor follows the Grande Randonnée coastal footpath along a shoreline that must surely be one of the most beautiful in the world, since this is Brittany's fabled 'Pink Granite Coast'. The inland section has some interesting churches and dolmens en route, as well as the exquisite wooded valley of the Traouiéros.

Start by walking along the road towards the sea, passing the Club Nautique, and turn left at the end of the road. Follow the white and red waymarks south, as you walk beside the sea, admiring your first view of the pink granite rocks which have given their name to this part of the coast. After 200m/yds turn left and walk beside the wall of a house. The waymarks are plentiful here, as they guide

The tiny oratory of St-Guirec on the Pink Granite Coast (Picnic 20)

you in front of houses and, in four minutes, towards boulders. Scramble upwards to where there is a variety of paths, with the GR34 marked every two or three metres. In two minutes turn left, either going down steps to the beach and walking along the beach to steps at the far end, or walking above the sand. Bear slightly left beyond the steps and pass to the right of a clump of trees in a garden.

The next bit is easy — a path leads you along the back of the beach. When it forks after a minute, bear right towards the markers and, in two minutes, go down to a little bay and bend eastwards. Walk beside the bay for nine minutes, making for a road ahead. The last 75m/yds on tarmac bring you to the junction with the D788 (**26min**).

Here you leave the GR34 for a while. Cross the road and walk up the Route du Dolmen opposite, following the signs 'Dolmen' and 'Allée Couverte'. Turn right in three minutes, along the Route du Kerguntuil. In another three minutes, ignore a track on the left. You approach some houses on the right. Over the hedge on your left, you can see the dolmen to which the signs referred. Beyond it you should be able to see the *allée couverte*, a kind of elongated dolmen. Follow the sign to view the dolmen (**37min**). Then leave the dolmen and continue in the same direction, turning left in two minutes at the crossroads. Some 50m/yds further on, turn left along a footpath, to have a look at the *allée cou-*

verte. Like the dolmen, it also would originally have been covered with earth.

Back on the road, turn left. In seven minutes ignore a road on the left, beside a farm but, after 100m/yds, turn left at a T-junction, for 'Trégastel'. Pass a road on your left in two minutes and, five minutes later, cross the D11 (**58min**). Walk up the road opposite, passing a cross on your right. In three minutes bear right at the top of the hill, to walk past the church (notice the tiny calvary). Beyond the church bear left at a fork for 'Perros Guirec', going to the left of the cemetery, war

Two shorter walks (grade and equipment as for main walk):

1 Trégastel-Plage — Trégastel — Vallée des Traouiéros — Trégastel-Plage (14.5km/9mi; 3h15min). 🚌 to Trégastel-Plage. Follow the main walk through the Vallée des Traouiéros. At the 1h31min-point, turn left and follow the road downhill. Some 50m/yds before the T-junction with the D788, turn left along a narrow road for 100m/yds. Cross the main road, turn left to cross the dam, and continue the main walk from the 3h17min-point.

2 Perros-Guirec — Ploumanac'h — Vallée des Traouiéros — Perros-Guirec (9.9km/6.1mi; 2h20min). 🚌 to Perros-Guirec: park at the Plage de Trestraou and follow the D788 behind it towards Ploumanac'h. When the road climbs away from the beach and turns sharply left, pick up the main walk notes at the 2h19min-point. Or drive along the D788 from Perros-Guirec towards Ploumanac'h, until the road turns sharp left (by a viewing platform). After 100m/yds turn right and follow the lane to a car park. Join the main walk at the 2h30min-point, by turning left as you face the sea. In either case, follow the main walk as far as the second dam (the 3h12min-point). Then cross the main road and turn left up a narrow tarmac road (beside a restaurant). After 100m/yds, turn right at a junction, and follow the road uphill for six minutes, to a notice board on the right: 'Site des Traouiéros'. Follow the path signposted 'Entrée-Chemin de Randreux', turning left at the bottom of steps. The path takes you to a small dam, where you turn right, and then left, to cross a stream and walk beside the lake. The woodland path criss-crosses the stream with its 'chaos' of boulders for a quarter of an hour, until you arrive at a sign, 'Sortie Panorama', which directs you to the left. Turn left, and the path will bring you up from the valley to a tarmac road. Turn left on the road and, after 100m/yds, take the first road on the right. Now continue back to your car by picking up the main walk notes at the 1h38min-point.

memorial, and water tower. Keep ahead by the cross and go downhill, past a road on the right.

At the bottom of the hill turn right (signposted 'Site Départemental Vallée des Traouiéros') and follow a footpath straight ahead (behind a cross; **1h09min**). When you cross a stream in a few metres/yards, take a close look at the macabre footbridge. Some 100m/yds beyond the stream the path forks. Uphill to the right a sign reads 'Sortie Panorama', but your way is to the left, parallel with the stream and in the direction of a 'chaos' of boulders ahead. Keep beside the stream for a quarter of an hour, crossing from one side to another, going over fallen trees and beneath fallen boulders, along this most delightful little valley. Occasionally you will pass paths leaving the valley to the right and left, but ignore them all. You will also pass a small cave. In 11 minutes you come to a small lake. At **1h24min** cross a footbridge over a stream that feeds it, and turn right to walk in front of the dam. Having turned left once more, in a couple of minutes you will see a sign ('Sortie de Chemin de Randreux'), pointing to steps on the right. Private property lies ahead: turn right here. Climb the steps and follow the path up the hill, to join a tarmac road. Just before the junction there is a fine picnic spot (**1h31min**). (*Shorter walk 1 turns left here.*)

Turn right here and follow the road gently uphill for seven minutes, as far as the first road on the left (**1h38min**). (*Shorter walk 2 rejoins the route of the main walk here.*) Turn left. Ahead you can see a quarry, which explains any explosions you may have heard. Go down the road, passing a small crossing lane. In six minutes you will be climbing to the left of the pink granite quarry — surely the most gorgeous building stone of all. Seven minutes later, at the top of the hill, keep straight ahead along the Rue des Carrières, ignoring two streets on the left and one on the right; then turn left on reaching a T-junction.

Carry on to the 16th-century chapel of Notre Dame de la Clarté, built in response to a vow. With his ship lost in fog, the Lord of Barac'h swore that if the Virgin would make a break in the fog, he would build her a chapel on the first piece of land he saw — hence its name: 'Our Lady of Light'. Turn right immediately beyond the chapel. Cross the D788 at the traffic lights (**2h04min**) and follow the Rue de la Clarté downhill, past several side turnings. Just beyond a little calvary on the right, the road bends left to descend to the Plage de Trestraou, Perros-Guirec's beach. (*This is the starting point for Shorter walk 2.*)

As it begins the final bend to the right, look out for a path on your left beside the 'Résidence la Roseraie', signposted 'Sentier des Douaniers'. You will also see the GR34 signpost and the white and red flashes, which will once more mark your route. Turn left along this footpath (**2h12min**). Walk between bracken-covered cliffs on the left and a craggy coast on the right, passing a track to the left after eleven minutes. (Five minutes later you may wish to detour up a path that climbs to the summit and viewing platform.) Two minutes later pass a campsite and car park. (*This is an alternative starting point for Shorter walk 2.*)

You are now at Ploumanac'h and, after 100m/yds, you will come upon the first masses of the great pink rocks and boulders for which it is famous (**2h32min**; *P*20). There are several tiny paths between the rocks and plenty of waymarks to guide you round the bay. This, too, is a wonderful place for a picnic. It will not be deserted, but the quality of the views will more than compensate for that! In ten minutes notice the remains of the *fortin* — a minuscule fort built to discourage pirates. Three minutes later, do not follow the track to the left (it leads to another car park), but keep on the path, beside a post. Soon waymarks lead you past the lifeboat station and into a park.

Four minutes after the lifeboat station, leave the Sentier des Douaniers (by a notice warning of its end and of a difficult passage 100m/yds ahead). Go to the left, following the GR waymarks, and head inland. In three minutes turn left, by a cross, to reach the beach of St-Guirec, where a tiny oratory stands on the sand in the middle of the bay (photograph pages 126-127). Turn right and walk across the back of the beach, in front of the Beau-Site Hotel. In four minutes, go up steps on the left; they bring you to a little chapel (**2h57min**). The waymarks lead you out of the churchyard, up more steps, and on between boulders. In three minutes turn left, passing in front of a shady area (a good picnic spot on a hot day). In another two minutes, turn left at a junction of paths. Four minutes later, you reach a tarmac road and Ploumanac'h town. Turn left.

Follow the promenade behind the port and turn right at the end of the bay, onto a roughly-tarred track which takes you across the dam. At the end of the dam, bear right and walk along the beach, until you come to the main road (D788; **3h17min**), just where it is about to go over a second dam. (*For Shorter walk 2, cross the road now, and turn left along a tiny tarmac road. Shorter walk 1 rejoins the route of the main walk at this point.*)

Turn right immediately beyond the dam, continuing to circle the harbour on a roughly-asphalted narrow lane. Go between houses and follow the lane round to the left. Turn right, when you come to a road junction, and walk to Tourony Beach. On the island ahead is the modern Château de Costaérès (photograph page 19), where Sienkiewicz wrote part of his epic of early Christianity, 'Quo Vadis?' (**3h25min**).

Turn left and walk round the back of the beach, then follow a track to the left, beneath cypress trees. Keep on the gravel track, and do not go into the wood. Soon sand comes underfoot, when you turn left and walk away from the beach. As the track narrows to footpath, you pass to the right of a lake and a splendid picnic site. Cross the dam and walk to the left of a hedge, away from the lake, towards tennis courts. Bear right at the first junction, then scramble down to the sand and walk round the back of the Bay of Ste-Anne for 15 minutes.

At the far side of the bay, turn right and follow the road in front of the Hôtel des Bains. After 500m/0.3mi, where the road bends left, turn right along a track. Go round a field, soon turning left to walk beside the beach once more (**4h**). You come to car parks and the lovely Ile Renote. Turn right along the causeway and follow the road through the car parks, then to the right.

The tarmac stops, and you bear right along the sandy Sentier des Douaniers. In two minutes the path turns left (signposted 'Chemin Piétonnier') and leads you past more splendid pink granite boulders. The path winds round the coast but, 12 minutes later, keep right, on the broader track. Three minutes afterwards, leave the wide track in favour of a narrow path to the right, which runs behind the superb beach. Having completed the circuit of the peninsula (**4h27min**), turn right and follow the GR-waymarked sandy track beside the last few metres of beach. After a minute turn left.

Cross another beach, then go up steps and along a narrow path to a car park, which you cross. Carry on along the pavement behind Coz Porz beach, then go down a slope and steps to a small concrete bridge. Follow the cliff path as it winds round to La Grève Blanche ('White Beach'), to which you descend by steps (**4h41min**). Walk along the beach to the far side, then follow the path round into the next bay, where almost at once you will see a road on the left by the Club Nautique. It leads you back to the car park where the walk began (**4h50min**).

BUS TIMETABLES

Quimper to Pont-Aven via La-Forêt and Concarneau (1h)
Depart Quimper (Place St-Corentin): weekdays 07.10 08.10 11.30 14.30 16.45 17.35 18.40; Sun/hols 08.35 11.30 14.00 18.40
Depart Pont-Aven: weekdays 06.30 08.15 10.15 12.45 17.15 18.10; Sun/hols 08.50 12.45 17.15 18.10

Quimper to St-Guénolé via Pont-l'Abbé (1h)
Depart Quimper (Place St-Corentin): weekdays 07.25 10.20 12.25 13.47 15.30 16.35 17.20 18.20 19.15; Sun/hols 07.25 10.20 13.47 15.30 17.20 20.45
Depart St-Guénolé: weekdays 07.00 08.40 11.45 13.00 13.45 15.00 17.00 18.30; Sun/hols 08.40 11.45 13.45 15.00 17.00 18.30

Quimper to Pointe du Raz (1h30min)
Depart Quimper (railway station): weekdays 08.00 11.05 16.00; Sun/hols 11.20 19.00
Depart Pointe du Raz: weekdays 08.00 12.00 15.50; Sun/hols 08.15 15.45

Quimper to Camaret (1h30min) via Locronan (20min), St-Nic (40min), Pentrez (43min), Crozon-Morgat (1h20min)
Depart Quimper (railway station): weekdays 07.15 (Mon) 09.40 13.35 17.55 19.05 (Fri); Sun/hols 09.40 13.35 17.55 20.40
Depart Camaret*: weekdays 05.10 (Mon) 11.25 15.40 17.10 (Fri); Sun/hols 08.00 11.25 15.40 17.00
Depart Crozon 10min later; depart Pentrez 38min later; depart St-Nic 42min later; depart Locronan 1h later

Brest to Camaret (1h20min) via Crozon-Morgat (1h10min)
Depart Brest: weekdays 12.00 (Mon-Fri) 18.45 (Mon, Wed, Fri) 13.15 (Sat)
Depart Camaret: weekdays 06.00 (Mon) 7.20 13.30 (Mon, Wed, Fri) 16.45 (hols)
Depart Crozon: weekdays 06.10 (Mon) 07.30 13.40 (Mon, Wed, Fri) 16.55 (hols)

Quimperlé to Pont-Aven (40min)
Depart Quimperlé (Quai Brizeuc): weekdays 06.00 (Place de la Gare) 07.35 09.35 12.00 15.30 17.30; Sun/hols 08.15 12.10 16.30 17.30
Depart Pont-Aven: weekdays 07.05 08.10 09.10 12.35 15.35 17.55 19.35; Sundays 09.35 12.35 15.05 19.35

Quimperlé to Le Faouët (30min)
Depart Quimperlé (Place de la Gare): weekdays 07.45 18.00 (except Sat)
Depart Le Faouët: weekdays 07.00 12.45 (except Sat)

Lorient to Le Faouët (1h)
Depart Lorient: weekdays 11.15 (Wed, Fri) 17.30 18.15 (except Sat)
Depart Le Faouët: weekdays 06.20 (except Sat) 07.45 12.45 (Fri) 13.00 (Wed)

Morlaix to Huelgoat (1h)
Depart Morlaix (railway station): weekdays 07.55 (Mon•) 08.30 (except Mon•) 14.30 (Wed, Sat) 18.30; Sundays 18.15
Depart Huelgoat: weekdays 06.25 12.30 (Wed Sat) 17.25 (except Wed•) 17.35 (Wed•); Sundays 17.05

Carhaix to Bon-Repos (1h)
Depart Carhaix: weekdays 09.25 13.00 16.15; Sundays 13.00 16.15
Depart Bon-Repos: weekdays 07.45 (except Sat) 09.40 (Sat) 13.15 16.35 18.45 (Fri); Sundays 16.25 20.55

Loudéac to Bon-Repos (30min)
Depart Loudéac: weekdays 07.15 (except Sat) 09.00 (Mon) 09.10 (Sat) 12.40 16.00 18.10 (Fri); Sundays 15.20 20.20
Depart Bon-Repos: weekdays 09.15 13.50 17.10; Sundays 16.55 19.35

Vannes to Carnac (1h20min)
Depart Vannes: 09.20 12.20 15.45 18.38 Depart Carnac: 10.40 13.50 16.35 19.06

Auray to Carnac (40min)
Depart Auray: 09.05 10.02 12.22 13.05 14.15 16.30 18.05 19.20
Depart Carnac: 08.30 09.58 10.40 12.25 13.50 16.35 17.13 19.06

Quiberon to Carnac (45min)
Depart Quiberon: 08.05 09.20 10.00 11.45 13.10 15.50 16.35 18.30
Depart Carnac: 09.51 10.40 13.03 13.43 14.59 17.07 18.47 19.56

■ term time only

Vannes to Josselin (1h)
Depart Vannes: weekdays 06.45 07.35 (Mon•) 16.30 18.20 (Fri•); Sun/hols 16.30
Depart Josselin: weekdays 06.40 (Mon•) 08.20 17.15 (Fri•) 18.39; Sun/hols 18.39

Vannes to Pontivy (1h20min)
Depart Vannes: weekdays 05.00 (Mon) 06.30 (Mon) 07.45 (Mon) 08.20 12.10 (except Wed, Sat•) 12.20 (Wed, Sat) 16.00 (except Wed, Sat) 17.50 (except Sat)
Depart Pontivy: weekdays 06.15 (Mon) 06.25 (except Mon) 06.50 (except term time) 07.40 (Mon) 07.45 (Mon) 08.00 12.10 (Wed) 12.30 (Sat) 13.00 (except Wed, Sat•) 13.15 (except term time) 16.20 (Mon-Fri except term time) 16.55 (except Sat) 17.30 (Fri)

Rennes to Josselin (2h) and Pontivy (1h45min)
Depart Rennes: weekdays 06.25 (Josselin only) 11.45 16.40 (Josselin only) 18.00 18.20 (Fri) 21.45 (except Fri) 22.20 (Fri); Sundays 16.40 (Josselin only) 20.00 (except holidays) 21.45
Depart Josselin: weekdays 06.35 07.45 11.25 14.25 17.31 18.40 (Fri); Sun/hols 15.10 (stops at STOC shop/RN24) 17.31 18.35 (stops at STOC shop/RN24)
Depart Pontivy: weekdays 0600 10.50 13.50 18.05 (Fri); Sun/hols 14.35 18.05

Auray to Pontivy (1h10min)
Depart Auray: weekdays 08.15 11.32 15.19 (Sat) 19.20; Sun/hols 11.32 15.19 19.20
Depart Pontivy: weekdays 06.50 09.55 13.05 17.10; Sun/hols 09.55 13.05 17.10

Loudéac to Pontivy (30min)
Depart Loudéac: weekdays 07.20 09.20 (except Sat) 12.05 (Sat) 15.25 17.00 (except Sat) 18.10 20.20 (except Fri) 20.30 (Fri); Sun/hols 15.25 20.20
Depart Pontivy: weekdays 06.40 07.55 (except Sat) 08.35 (Sat) 12.30 16.30 (except Sat) 17.35 18.45; Sun/hols 12.30 17.00

Lorient to Pontivy (1h20min)
Depart Lorient: weekdays 06.20 (Mon) 07.25 13.00 16.15 (except Wed, Sat) 17.05 (except term time; Wed, Sat•); Sundays 19.30
Depart Pontivy: weekdays 06.20 (Mon) 07.40 13.20 17.00

St-Malo to Dinan (50min)
Depart St-Malo: weekdays (except holidays) 08.30 12.15 (Wed, Sat•) 13.25 18.10
Depart Dinan: weekdays (except holidays) 06.50 10.10 (Wed, Sat•) 12.30 17.00

Dinard to Dinan (30-50min)
Depart Dinard: weekdays 06.53 07.05 08.42 (Thur) 09.00 11.18 (Wed, Sat) 11.35 (except Sat) 13.10 13.30 (except Sat) 14.20 (Sat•) 16.00 (Fri•) 17.50; Sun/hols 09.00 17.50 21.15 (•)
Depart Dinan: weekdays 07.40 (Mon•) 07.43 (except Mon•) 08.00 09.41 12.13 12.25 (Wed, Thur, Sat) 12.53 (Fri•) 13.28 14.58 16.45 (except Wed, Sat) 17.52 (Sat•) 19.11; Sun/hols 12.13 19.11 20.39 (•)

Rennes to Dinan (1h15min)
Depart Rennes: weekdays 06.20 (Mon) 06.35 (except Mon) 09.40 11.00 11.45 (Fri•) 13.45 16.45 (except Sat) 18.00; Sun/hols 11.00 18.00 19.30 (•)
Depart Dinan: weekdays 06.30 07.40 09.37 12.30 (Sat•) 13.42 14.55 (except Sat) 16.30 (Fri • 18.27; Sun/hols 09.37 18.27 21.45 (•)

TRAIN TIMETABLES

Morlaix to St-Thégonnec (15min) and Guimiliau (20min)
Depart Morlaix: weekdays 06.30 (except Sat) 07.42 12.35 16.43 (Fri) 17.13 (except Fri, Sat) 18.18; Sun/hols 18.18
Depart St-Thégonnec (trains depart from Guimiliau five minutes earlier): weekdays 07.37 13.07 17.27 18.07 (except Sat) 19.01 (except Sat); Sun/hols 16.04

Brest to St-Thégonnec (40min) and Guimiliau (35min)
Depart Brest: weekdays 06.57 12.28 16.41 17.28 (except Sat) 18.15 (except Sat); Sun/hols 15.25
Depart St-Thégonnec (trains depart from Guimiliau five minutes later): weekdays 06.44 (except Sat) 07.56 12.50 16.56 (Fri) 17.26 (except Fri, Sat) 18.31; Sun/hols 18.32

Dol to Dinan (25min)
Depart Dol: 07.24 (except Sun/hols) 10.12 (except Sun/hols) 10.16 (Sun) 11.23 (Sun) 12.20 (except Sat, Sun/hols) 12.23 (Sat, Sun/hols) 14.27 17.35 18.14 20.23 20.51 22.22 (Sat) 23.08 (Fri, Sun/hols)
Depart Dinan: 05.45 (Mon) 06.39 (except Sun/hols) 07.52 11.33 (except Sat, Sun, July, Aug) 12.56 13.50 13.51 16.15 (Fri) 16.46 (except Sat, Sun) 16.48 (Sat, Sun) 18.48
•in term time only

❋ Index

eographical names comprise the only entries in this Index. For other
tries see Contents, page 3. A page number in *italic type* indicates a
ap; a page number in **bold type** indicates a photograph or sketch.
oth of these may be in addition to a text reference on the same page.

er Benoît (estuary) 11, 20
(river) **18**, 111, 113, *114-15*
couest, Pointe de l' 41
gent (river) *62*, 64
ée, Monts d' 4, 23, 25, 70, *72-3*
dierne 13, 29
lne (river) 23, 24, 26
ray 14, 20, 31, 34, 133, 134
en (river) 90, *91*, 92

ud 31
Baule 4, 7
Baussaine 42
auport, Abbaye de 39, 41
cherel 42, 45
lle-Isle-en-Terre 40
nodet 7, 28
rven 21
ven-Assis, Château de 44
uzy 32
vet (river) 13, 14, 32, 106, 107,
108-9, 122, *123*, 125
is d'Amour 90, *91*
n-Repos, Abbaye du 14, **24**, 32,
122, *123*, **125**, 126, 133
urbansais, Château de la 42, 43
asparts 26, 72
annilis 26
Lac de — 72, 74
est 4, 6, 7, 11, 17, 53, 106, 133,
134
Canal see under Nantes
eton Corniche 39, 41, 127
ézal, Moulin de 18
gnogan-Plage 22
océliande, Forêt de 35, 110, *114*
öns 45

maret-sur-Mer 12, **23**, 24, 52,
54, 56, 133
mp d'Artus (site) *62*, 64
radeuc, Château de 45
rantec 11
rhaix 133
rnac 8, 34, 93, *94*, 95, **96**, 133
Chapelle Chaussée 45
artreuse, Abbaye de la 31
âteaugiron 42
âteaulin 26
âteaulaudren 40
Châtenay 36, 113, *114*
Ciarté 15
Ciarté, N-D de (chapel) *129*,
130
der 22
mbourg 43
mmana 25
ncarneau 27, 28, 133

Confort 30
Le Conquet 11, 19
Cornouaille ('Cornwall') 27, 86
Costaérès, Château de **19**, *129*,
132
Côte de Granit Rose 4, **19**, 39, 41,
126-7, *128-9*, 131, 132
Côtes-d'Armor 39, 42, 116, 127
Coz Porz (beach) *128*, 132
Crozon 23, 57, 133

Daoulas 25
Gorges du — 14, 32, 122, *123*,
125, 126
Dinan 7, 15, **21**, 43, 116, **117**, *118*,
120, 121, 134
Anse de Dinan 23, 55
Château de Dinan (rock forma-
tions) 23
Dinard 7, 134
Dol-de-Bretagne 134
Douarnenez 30, 88
Le Drennec 75, *77*
Barrage du — (lake) 75, 76, 77

Elez (river) 26, 72, 74
Ellé (river) 33, 101, **102-3**, *105*
Elorn (river) 17, 18, 25, 75, *76-7*
Elven 38
Espagnols, Pointe des 24

Le Faou 25
Le Faouët 14, 31, 33, 101, 104,
105, 133
Finistère 4, 7, 17, 23, 27, 29, 47,
53, 57, 61, 65, 75, 78, 83, 87
Le Folgoët 17, 20, 21, 22
La Forêt-Fouesnant 28, 133
Fouesnant 28
Fougères 43
Fréhel, Cap 44

Le Géant (menhir) **20**, *94*
Le Gorvello 36
Goulven 22
Grand Menhir, Le 34
La Grève Blanche 127, *128*, 132
Grillemont, Château de 117, *118*,
120, **121**
Guéhenno 9, 35, 38
Guerlédan, Lac du 14, 32
Guimiliau 17, 48, *49*, 51, 134
Guincamp 39, 40
Gurunhuel 40

Hennebont 33
Huelgoat 4, 12, **13**, 23, 26, **60**, 61,
62, 113, 133

Les Iffs 45
Ile Renote, L' *129*, 132
Ile-Grand, L' 15
Ille-et-Vilaine 42

Josselin 14, 35, 37, 97, *100*, 134
Jugon-les-Lacs 45

Kerampeulven, Menhir de 61, *62*,
63
Kercado, Château de *94*, 95
Kerfons, Chapelle de 39
Kergrist, Château de 39
Kerguehennec Sculpture Park 35,
38
Kérinec, N-D de (chapel) 30
Kerjean, Château de 20, 21
Kerlescan, Alignements de *94*, 95
Kerloas, Menhir de 19
Kermaria-an-Iskuit (chapel) 39, 40
Kermario, Alignements de 93, *94*,
96
Kérouzéré, Château de 22
Kerpenhir, Pointe de 14
Kervignac 33
Kreisker, Chapelle du 21, 22

Lagatjar, Alignements de 24, 52,
53, *54*
Lamballe 44
Lampaul-Guimiliau 17
Landerneau 17, 18, 25
Landivisiau 17, 18, 75
Landujan 45
Langonnet, Abbaye de 33
Lannion 39, 41,
Largoët, Fortresse de see Tours
d'Elven
Latte, Fort de la **2**, 44
Léguer (river) 39
Léhon 116, *118*, 120
Léon 17, 25, 48
Lesneven 21, 22
Liscuis, Allées couvertes de 122,
123, 126
Locmariaquer 14, 34
Locquénolé 11, 22
Locronan 30, 78, **79**, *80*, 81, 82,
133
Lorient 7, 133, 134
Lost Mar'ch 12, *58*, 60
Point de — 12, *58*, 60
Loudéac 133, 134
Louvigné 43
Luzec, Calvaire de 48, *49*, 50

Malestroit 36
La Martyre 25

135

Men-Du, Plage du *94*, 96
Le Ménec 93, *94*
    Alignements du Ménec 93, *94*
Ménez-Hom (hill) 12, 23, 65, 66, *67*, 69
Ménez-Mikel (hill) 13, 26, 72, *73*, **74**
Merlevenez 33
Miroir des Fées (pond) 110, *114*
Mont-St-Michel, Le (island) 16
Montagnes Noires ('Black Mountains') 4
Montauban, Château de 45
Montmuran, Château de 45
Morbihan 31, 34, 35, 97, 101, 106
    Golfe du — 4, 7, 14, 31, 34, 35
Morgat 12, 23, 57, *58*, 60
Morlaix 6, 11, 17, 22, 133, 134
Moros (river) 27, 28
Mougau, Allée Couverte du 25
Mur-de-Bretagne 14, 32

Nantes 4, 6, 106
    Canal de Nantes à Brest **17**, 32, 106, *108-9*, 122, *123*, **125**
Névet, Forêt de 78, *80*, 81
Nizon *91*

Odet (river) 28
Oust (river) 15, 36, 97, *100*

Paimpol 41
Paimpont 15, 36, 113
    Forêt de — 4, 36, 110, 113, *114-15*
Palue, Plage de la **56-7**, *58*, 59, 60
Parc Naturel Régional d'Armorique 23, 70, *72-3*
Pen-Hat, Anse de 12, 24, 52, 53, *54*
Pen-Hir, Pointe de 12, 23, 24, 52, 53, *54*, 59
Penmarc'h 13, 28, 83, *84*, 85
Pentrez, Plage de 65, *66*, 68, 133
Penzé (river) 22, 48, *49*, 51
Perros-Guirec 7, 15, 41, *129*, 130
Phare d'Eckmühl (lighthouse) 28, 83
Pierres-Plats (dolmen) 14
'Pink Granite Coast' *see under* Côte
Plas ar Horn **8**, 78, *80*
Plessis-Josso, Château de 36
Pleugueneuc 42, 43
Pleyben 9, 26
Ploërmel 35, 36, 37
Plogoff 27, 29
Ploudiry 25

Plouescat 22
Ploumanac'h 15, 41, *129*, 131
Plozévet 29
Plumelec 38
Pont-Aven 27, 90, *91*, 133
Pont-Croix 29
Pont-l'Abbé 28, 133
Pontivy 32, 106, *109*, 134
Porz (Pors) Carn 29, 83, *84*

Queffleuth (river) 61
Quénécan, Forêt de 14, 122, *123*
Questembert 36
Quiberon 14, 31, 35, 133
Quimper 6, 7, 13, 27, 30, 133
Quimperlé 33, 133
Quintin 40

Rance (river) 7, 15, 116, **117**, *118-9*, 120, **121**
Raz, Pointe du 29, 30, 86, 88, *89*, 133
Rennes 6, 42, 45, 97, 134
Roc'h Toull 48, *49*, 50, 51
Roc'h Trédudon 26
Roc'h Trévézel 25
Rocamadour, N-D de (chapel) 52, *54*
Roche aux Fées, La **1**, 42
Roche Tremblante, La 61, *62*
La Roche-Maurice 18
Rochefort-en-Terre 35, 36
Roscoff 6
Rostrenen 32
Rustéphan, Château de *91*, **92**

St-Fiacre (chapel) 14, 33, 101, 103, *105*
St-Gildas-de-Rhuys 35
St-Guénolé 13, 29, 83, *84*, 133
    Musée de Préhistoire 29, 83, *84*, 85
St-Guirec 15, **126-7**, *129*, 131
St-Jean-Brévelay 38
St-Jean-Trolimon 29
St-Magloire, Abbaye *118*, 120
St-Malo 6, 7, 134
St-Mathieu, Pointe de 11, 19, 53
St-Nic 12, 65, *66*, 68, 133
St-Nicodème (chapel) 32
St-Nicolas-des-Eaux 13, 32
St-Norgard **22**, *58*, 59
St-Pol-de-Léon 21, 22
St-Rivoal 26, 70, **71**, *72-3*, 74
St-Thégonnec 17, 48, *49*, **50**, 51, 134
St-They (chapel) **86**, 87, *89*
St-Tugen (chapel) 29

Ste-Anne-d'Auray 31
Ste-Barbe (chapel) 33, 101, *105*
Ste-Marie-du-Ménez-Hom 23, 65, *67*, 69
Sedon (river) 97-99, *100*
Sizun **9**, **24**, 25, 75, *76*, 77
    Cap —, Bird Sanctuary 30, 86
Stival 106, *108*, 109
Sucinio, Château de 35

Table des Marchands (dolmen) 34
Taden 15, *118*, 120
Tas de Pois 24, 52, 54, 59
Ti ar Boudiked (dolmen) 26
Tinténiac 42
Tonquédec, Château de 39
Torche, Pointe de la 13, 29, **82**, 83, *84*, 85
La Touche-Trébry, Château de la 44
Tours d'Elven, Les 38
Traouiéros, Vallée des 127, *129*, 130
Trébeurden 15, 41
Trécesson, Château de 36
Trédion 38
    Château de **cover photograph**
Trégastel-Plage 41, 127, *128-9*, 132
Tréglonou 11, 20
Tréguier 41
Tréhorenteuc 15, 37, 110, *114*
Trémalo (chapel) 91
Trémazan 20
    Château de — 20
Trépassés, Baie des 30, 86, 87, *89*
Trestraou, Plage de *129*, 130
Trieux (river) 39, 41
La Trinité-sur-Mer 34
Tronoën (Tronoan)
    Plage de 83, *84*
    N-D de (chapel) 29, 83, *84*
Tumiac (tumulus) 34

La **Val** au Houx (farm) 97, 99, *100*
Val Sans Retour, Le 37, 110, 111, **112**, 113, *114*
Van, Pointe du **86**, 88, *89*
Vannes 35, 38, 133, 134
Vauban, Tour de **23**, 52, *54*
Vénus de Quinipily 31
Veryarc'h, Plage 52, *54*
Vilaine (river) 43
Vitré 42, 43

Yeun Elez 13, 26, *73*, 74